THE BEALE PAPERS

Presenting details of an alleged burial of gold, silver and jewels
near Goose Creek, Bedford, County, Virginia, by
Thomas Jefferson Beale and associates in
November 1819 and December 1821.

By

George L. Hart, Sr.

In an attempt to bring up-to-date
all that is known and surmised about the subject.
Being printed for the first time since 1964.

Edited with an introduction by

Brett Warren

Esoterica Press

2019

The Beale Papers
by George L. Hart in 1964,

This First Edition is made from the original manuscript
available at the Roanoke Public Library, VA.

Esoterica Press

Part of a collection from
The Beale Cipher Library

Edited with an Introduction by Brett Warren
Manufactured in the United States

www.esotericapress.com

ISBN: 978-1-952658-01-3

To the Intrigued Reader

In 1885 a curious pamphlet was printed. The contents of which were contrived of an infamous historic tract, entitled *The Beale Papers.* The contents of its pages would become the primary source of a historic legend, detailing the narrative of a treasure amounting to a modern estimate of $20 million in gold, silver and jewels. Buried somewhere in the Virginian county of Bedford in 1819 was yet enlarged with a second deposit in 1821. The narrative speaks of a mysterious figure who led the party responsible for the treasure's burial, a man named Thomas Jefferson Beale. After the burial, Beale wrote a series of letters detailing the origin of the treasure and included with them three pages of cipher text containing secret instructions to of the treasure's contents, the location of the treasure, and the list of heirs to which portions of the treasure would be distributed. While the party buried this treasure, they stayed at the inn of a Mr. Robert Morriss. But before departing, Beale left these papers with Morriss and was never heard from again. Though Morriss attempted to eventually solve the ciphers himself, only one cipher was solved using the Declaration of Independence as the Key.

These papers have been studied and challenged by several prominent academics, researchers, cryptologists, mathematicians, and historians since they were first made public in 1885. It was such that a stenographer by the name of Clayton I. Heart had attempted to decode the ciphers and, near the year of 1897, had learned that one James B. Ward of Campbell County had discovered the key to one cipher but later abandoned his efforts to solve the others, prompting him to publish the letters. Clayton journeyed to Lynchburg,

Va., 50 miles east of Roanoke, to secure a copy of the printed pamphlet and consult Ward about his knowledge. Clayton was informed that although the manuscript was printed in Lynchburg by the Virginian Job Print, all but a few copies of the original pamphlets had been destroyed in a fire that broke out at the printing plant. This occurred prior to the plan of its distribution and the sale of 50¢ per copy was able to be carried out. It may seem from the outset that such an occurrence may allude to an operation to sabotage its printing, to thereby cease the dissemination of this curious tract. In 1903, Clayton met with Ward, who confirmed his narrative of the pamphlet in person. Clayton and his brother attempted to both decode the cipher and traverse the Blue Ridge Mountains to discover the location of the treasure, to no avail, for a number of decades.

In December of 1924, some years after the passing of Clayton I. Hart, his brother George Clayton learned of the success of one Colonel George Fabyan, whom had since become a famed cryptographer in World War I and had also managed a laboratory. George contacted Fabyan and sent a copy of the pamphlet through correspondence to inquire his expertise on the matter.

Although George Clayton relates that he had not heard from Fabyan since, it would so happen that many other researchers soon followed. In the mid-1900s, The Beale Cypher Association (BCA) was established "as a not-for-profit scientific association having its principal office in Medfield, Massachusetts, and sponsoring a research and investigation program pertaining to the Beale Ciphers."[1] The association was comprised of about 100 members and held esteemed experts as Dr. Carl Hammer, director of computer sciences at Sperry Univac; Per A. Holst, senior research manager at the Foxboro Company; and top cryptanalysts of

---

[1] Beale Cypher Association Membership Application. See NSA Doc ID: 656736.

the CIA, including Carl Nelson Jr., who was a mastermind behind the top-secret Berlin tunnel, dug to intercept the communications of Communist officials.[2] BCA members organized collaborative research efforts to decipher the texts, to which their contributions earned them points towards a share of the treasure if found.[3] These efforts were supplemented with a flow of letters amounting to more than 10,000 posted to the office of BCA's Executive Director Per Holst (though most were simple requests for information by curious citizens).[4] The BCA compiled a comprehensive 'Research Library' comprised of the many books, reports, cryptography software, and memoranda concerning the Beale Ciphers whilst offering cryptanalysis services.[5]

Efforts to locate the treasure did not stop at the attempt to decode the ciphers, but even included endeavors to discover the identity of the mysterious Thomas Jefferson Beale through genealogical record and researching old newspaper advertisements to discover details around the formation of his party.[6] However, after nearing a century since the initial publication of the ciphers, David Khan, author of Codebreakers, declared in 1972 his belief that the papers were nothing more than an elaborate hoax.[7] Although some have shared this sentiment,[8] others were in agreement with the earlier statement of George Fabyan outlined above, as

---

[2] Ruth Daniloff (ND). A cipher's key to the treasure in them thar hills. *Smithsonian*. 126-144. NSA Doc ID: 656765.

[3] Beale Cypher Association Research Library Catalogue. NSA Doc ID: 656765.

[4] Ruth Daniloff. A Cipher's the key to the treasure... *Smithsonian*. 126-144.

[5] Beale Cypher Association Membership Application. NSA Doc ID: 656736.

[6] Carl W. Nelson (1972). *Historical and Analytical Studiesin Relation to the Beale Cyphers.* A Report to the Beale Cyphers Study Committee (BCSC). NSA Doc ID: 656726; See also Carl W. Nelson (1970). *Historical and Analytical studies in Relation to the Beale Cyphers*. NSA Doc ID: 656725. Being a prepublication study of the BCSC.

[7] BSA Research Library Catalogue.

[8] Louis Kruh (1988). The Beale Cypher as a Bamboozlement. Part I. *Cryptologia XII*(4). 241-246. Found as NSA Doc ID: 656729.

Carl Hammer himself admitted, "With a key, a second grader could decode the Beale Ciphers." Supposing a key does exist, reporter Ruth Daniloff recounts an estimate of earlier historians that it may lie within some 2000 books and early government documents that Beale may have had access to at the time; though the common go-to mentions have been Shakespeare's works, the Bible, the Magna Carta, and other historical documents dating back to the 1600s.[9] Though news of the treasure had somewhat subsided some decades following the hype of the BCA's endeavors, a recent Freedom of Information Act request lead to the declassification and release of a plethora of the aforementioned reports and studies of The Beale Papers in 2001, held by the National Security Agency (NSA).

With all the controversy and fame that this story has received throughout the past century, none have alluded to the success of this legendary treasure's discovery. Even to this modern day, none have been able to come publicly forward to legitimately provide a key that solves the riddle within these pages; nor has one given the public proof that the treasure has been discovered or claimed. Are these ciphers an unbreakable code without the required key? Or are the papers simply a centuries old American hoax meant to turn a profit in pamphlet sales? Whatever the truth of the matter may be, this document is a mysterious piece of early American history that is enveloped with such mystery that hundreds, if not thousands, of men have dedicated decades of countless hours of their lives to solve the puzzle; or to traverse in search within the wilderness of Bedford County; with the small yet ever lingering string of hope that one may come to discover the immense fortune of the infamous Beale Treasure.

The following work, composed by George L. Heart, has only seven known original copies in the form of manuscripts

---

[9] Ruth Daniloff. A Cipher's the Key to the treasure… *Smithsonian*. 126-144.

that were distributed to seven different libraries. This edition is derived from the type-written manuscript held at the Roanoke Public Library located in Roanoke, Va. It is now published for the first time since its printing in 1964. Transcribed in full; line by line and word for word. It is but a true account of the decades-long journey that two brothers shared in attempting to find a lost but legendary American treasure. Yet when their skill in the scientific art of cryptography failed to prove useful, their desperation did lead them to turn to other more paranormal devices and to no avail. It is a grand look into the historical perspective upon such a treasure; and the lengths some were willing to go to find it. If any may be so inclined to study the papers themselves, may the intrigued reader learn from the faults of these brothers. The work is published for the first time and contains the contents of the Beale Papers within, edited by the author, George L. Heart; with added details of the history of these papers and the cryptographic analysis from the research he conducted with his brother.

Brett Warren

August 10, 2019

THE BEALE PAPERS.

Presenting details of an alleged burial of gold, silver and jewels near Goose Creek, Bedford, County, Virginia, by Thomas Jefferson Beale and associates in November 1819 and December 1821.

By

George L. Hart, Sr.

In an attempt to bring up-to-date all that is known and surmised about the subject.

As of the present date, January 1, 1952, the writer will make an effort to put in writing all that he knows or surmises about the above subject, study and work upon which he spent many hours, days, a total of many months, extending over a period from 1898 to 1922, more or less in collaboration with his brother, the late Clayton I. Hart, of Roanoke, Virginia.

Along in the summer of 1897 my brother, then a stenography to the office of the Auditor of the Norfolk & Western Railroad, Roanoke, Va., was requested by the chief clerk to the Auditor Mr. Hazlewood, then residing at Montvale, (formerly Buford) Buford County, Virginia, to make several copies of eight sheets of notepaper, two sheets headed simply "No.1", three sheets headed "No.2", and three sheets headed "No.3".

Curiosity impelled Clayton to ask Mr. Hazlewood what such figures, most unusual in his experience in the office, could possibly mean. In the beginning of their conversation

Mr. Hazlewood related that they were connected with a treasure, said to have been buried some four score years before near the foot of the Peaks of Porter, which stood in all their majesty overlooking his residence; so that, as far as he knew, said treasure had never been located. Clayton obtained permission to retain a copy of the three ciphers or cryptograms.

Clayton immediately began studying the meaningless figures, discussing with Mr. Hazlewood from time to time this or that possibility; however, neither getting anywhere near the beginning of a solution. In a few months Mr. Hazlewood's health began to fail, whereupon he expressed an intention to give no further attention to the mystery, passing it on to Clayton with the admonition:

"Go ahead on your own. I wish you success. Even though I have never made any headway in the matter of deciphering the figures, I remain reasonably confident the treasure lies buried where originally placed."

About that time Clayton learned that a man by the name of Ward had spent many years trying to find a key, or keys, to the ciphers; that he had found a key to one cipher, but had finally abandoned his efforts and published in pamphlet form all that he knew about the treasure.

Thereupon, Clayton journeyed to Lynchburg, Va., 50 miles east of Roanoke, secured a copy of the printed pamphlet, and redoubled his efforts to find a solution.

The manuscript which will follow this foreword was prepared by James B. Ward, of Campbell County, Virginia, contiguous to Lynchburg, in the year 1885. It was printed in pamphlet form by the Virginian Job Print, Lynchburg, Va. However, Clayton was informed by Ward that all but a few copies had been destroyed by fire, which broke out in the printing plant before a plan of distribution and sale at 50¢ a copy had been made and carried out.

About the year 1903 Clayton visited Mr. Ward, who then was at an advanced age. He confirmed all that is contained in the pamphlet; and his son, then U.S. Mail transfer clerk at the union station, Lynchburg, added his own confirmation, but in somewhat sad and solemn terms. Both are long since deceased.

They put in practically every moment of their spare time in an effort to find a key, or keys, for the two ciphers which are as yet meaningless. Residing then in Roanoke, Va., fourteen miles west of Montvale, (formerly Buford) Bedford County, Virginia, frequent trips were made by one or other of us, both of us together sometimes, to the supposed general location of the alleged buried treasure. And, on visits to Lynchburg, whence we journeyed occasionally on professional work, we secured confirmation as to the Washington Hotel, and its proprietor, Mr. Moriss, during the period 1819 to 1862.

My brother and I, separately and jointly, turned to the Constitution, Shakespeare, the Declaration of Independence, and numerous other books and documents that we thought might have been in the library of the Washington Hotel, at Lynchburg, during Beale's sojourn there. We numbered the words forward and backward. Finally skipping the first word and beginning with the second, then starting with the third word, fourth and fifth words, then taking every fifth word, tenth word, etc. However, we found no solution.

In 1898 my brother Clayton became interested in mesmerism and hypnotism. He wondered if this might be the means of securing a lead. Finding an excellent subject, who gradually drifted into crystal reading, Clayton began questioning him about the alleged treasure. Thinking he was, by this means, securing a worthwhile lead, Clayton asked the writer to sit in on a séance. The result of the sitting will be given in detail near the end of this story. Of course, the writer, then as now, placed no faith in what came forth so glibly from the mouth of the crystal reader. But, like a drowning man, we were catching at any straws that might float about.

So, when the subject, during his trance, claimed he could see not only the alleged buried treasure, but would be able to lead us to it, we determined to test him out.

One nice spring evening in 1899, the writer and his brother departed from Roanoke about five o'clock p.m. in the family buggy, drawn by the faithful family horse, Old Nell. We carried what we believed to be the necessary equipment including picks, shovels, lanterns, rope, an axe, etc. And with us, of course, was out confident crystal reader—that is, confident to the Nth degree when he was gazing into the crystal ball.

We drove by "The Great Lick", a mile to the east of old homestead, which, it is claimed, in the colonial days attracted wild animals desiring salt, on east through the gap of the Blue Ridge Mountains, to the tavern location in the village known in 1819-22 as Buford, (now Montvale) said tavern supposed to have been visited by Beale and his associates while seeking a place to bury the alleged treasure, and the subsequent trip.

Darkness had settled over the land, as we had expected, and which the better suited our purpose. Few people were moving about, and the faint light o a receding moon afforded opportunity to see objects of any size, which was just what we wanted.

Driving across the railroad track, in the direction of the Peaks of Otter, we stopped on reaching a clump of bushes and many trees, about a mile up Goose Creek. My brother and the subject alighted, the subject hypnotized, and they started off along Goose Creek I following in the buggy. The trail led toward a gap in the mountain that would, if followed, take on over into Botetourt County.

And so not be amiss to pause here and explain, that in the town of Buchanan, just over the mountain, there lived a quite prominent family of the name of Beale, who owned a plantation bordering on James River.

But, to resume our narrative: About four miles up Goose Creek the subject stopped, seemed to be taking his bearings, then climbed a rail fence, jumped across a spring brand, ascended a hill, walked over the top and down into a crater-like place, covered with old oak trees and many leaves. Halting by the side of a large oak the subject pointed to the ground at its base and exclaimed: "There's the treasure! Can't you see it?"

Well, had we finally reached the promised land? We did not believe it possible, and yet there was a certain plausibility about the confidence of the subject, so we took stock of our situation and planned our work. Lighting another lantern, we placed one on each side of the spot, to judge how much of the light from our lanterns might be seen in the neighborhood.

Satisfied of our safety from intrusion, we agreed that each brother would dig, or shovel, for 10 minutes, then to be relieved by the other brother. This was to be continued until we located the treasure, or were satisfied that it was not there. In the meantime the subject was relieved of his trance, and he lay down in the leaves, apparently wondering what we were about, but otherwise showing no interest.

We diligently set to work digging. After some six hours or more, in the wee small hours of the following morning, we had succeeded in digging a hole approximately six feed in depth, and slight larger than a grave. Our strength was about gone, we were filled with misgivings, and, then, when about 8 of the ten minutes of my brother's turn had been used, his pick struck a rock that produced a hollow sound. He looked up at me, his eyes flashing the fire of hope, and I, in my own enthusiasm, said: "You're played out! Permit me to relieve you now!" But, no, he replied: "Let me finish my allotted time."

After awhile we succeeded in removing the rock, but the hoped-for pots of gold and silver were not underneath it. Now, were we let down? To relieve our chagrin the subject was again hypnotized and asked to reveal the whereabouts of the treasure. Rising on the balls of his feet, as if in disgust, he pointed to the left about two feet, directly underneath the great oak tree, and exclaimed: "There it is! You got over too far! Can't you see it?"

Thereupon I was completely let-down, and unwilling to make any further attempt, certainly so far as that trip was concerned. Crestfallen, we wended our way back home. A week or two later my brother returned to the spot alone, I refusing to accompany him. He provided himself with dynomite, and upon his return home he informed me that he blasted out the old tree, and about everything near it—but, still no pots of gold, silver and jewels.

Was there anything more that we should and could do? After a short lapse of time my brother and I held a conference. We reviewed all that we had done, or attempted to do, and tried to map out a plan of future action, if any, we should take. We agreed that we had never heard that a person could transfer to the mind of a hypnotized subject, his own beliefs or knowledge, and got the subject to repeat them; yet we wondered if, after all, that I had never been anywhere near the spot to which the subject led us; nor had he any thought that Beale and his party had gone there while seeking a place to hide the treasure. So, why did the subject now lead us to that spot? We could not then, nor do we now, find any satisfactory answer. Like many other questions that flash through one's mind, there seems no way to turn in the hope of getting the mystery cleared up.

Subsequent to my visit to the spot pointed out by the subject, I gave less and less time to a study of the ciphers; and, about 1912, I ceased altogether. Clayton, on the other hand, made many visits to the spot, and continued his interest in the ciphers until his death September 6, 1949.

In 1949 I moved to Washington, D.C., and began the practice of my profession in that city, where, until 1946, I was extremely busy, night and day. So, after 1919, I only gave casual thought to the subject; now and then going back and reading over my old papers, and writing some one, or talking with someone about it.

In the December, 1924, number of THE AMERICAN I read an article about Colonel George Fabyan, of Riverbank Laboratories, Geneva, Ill., and his success during World War I, and since, in reading coded messages. I wrote to him, sending a copy of the three ciphers; and, after some correspondence back and forth, I forwarded to him a copy of such data as I had, but with special request that he not make any use of the manuscript, or ciphers, other than an attempt to decipher the ciphers. I made this request because my brother Clayton, then living, was trying to prepare something for publication, which he never did.

Under date of February 3, 1925, Colonel Fabyan replied, and, among other things of no special interest to me, said:

"*Now, in reference to the three ciphers: It seems improbable to us that a cipher of this character could be deciphered by a novice without the key, regardless of whether he put 20 years or 40 years on it. The cipher would be classified as a complex substitution cipher---variable key system, or pseudo code; and even though one were told that the Declaration of Independence was the key, unless it was intimated as to how it was used as a key, we think that the novice would have been utterly baffled as to how to use it. The stumbling of a novice upon a method of this character lies rather beyond the range of possibility, and the conviction follow that they were in possession of the key of not only No.2, but also of No.1 and No.3, with the result that the treasure referred to has long since been removed and converted.*"

"*I repeat, that the problem has my interest, and I am writing in the vain hope that either you or Clayton I. Hart can give us further information, because the psychology of it is about all we have to go on in picking out our point of attack. In the meantime we will retain the pamphlet, and work on it as we can find time to do so.* "

But I never heard further from Colonel Fabyen, and assume that he was unable to do anything toward clearing up the mystery.

As I often said to my brother, and wrote to Colonel Fabyen, it is possible the whole thing is without basis. I have wondered if Ward might have written his manuscript based on some figures he found, or made up; and yet, we have the word of Ward, his son, and friends to the contrary. Inquiry among some aged neighbors of Ward showed the high respect they had for him, and brought forth the statement that Ward would never practice deception.

Just as a little sidelight on the ramifications of this work, I will add the following: In 1917 my wife asked me to drive her to town for a visit to her cousin, Mr. Otey, near Montvale, formerly Buford. On arrival at Montvale we were directed to drive along Goose Creek, cross that stream at the first crossing, and drive up the other side, when we would reach Mr. Otey's place. All of which we did. While sitting out on the porch enjoying a glass of lemonade, I remarked that some years before I had had occasion to to drive up the old road, on the other side of the creek, in a buggy. Being asked the occasion for such a visit, I told him the story of our digging. He laughed, loud and long, telling me it cleared up a mystery that had worried the people along the creek for upwards of 20 years. He stated that after the first hole we dug was discovered, some of his neighbors watched all night for a few days, armed with shotguns; and that after what was described as "the great explosion", a watch was again set for a week or 10 days, without result.

I have often wondered what became of the key, or keys, to the ciphers, left by Beale with some friend in St. Louis, when he was there in 1822, and visited the Planters Hotel.

The following is what Ward wrote, and had printed in pamphlet form, about the Beale Papers:

"THE BEALE PAPERS

"The following details of an incident that happened many years ago, but which has lost none of its interest on that account, are now given to the public for the first time.

"Until now, for reasons which will be apparent to every one, all knowledge of this affair was confined to a very limited circle -- to the writer's immediate family, and to one old and valued friend, upon whose discretion he could always rely; nor was it ever intended that it should travel beyond that circle; but circumstances over which he has no control, pecuniary embarrassments of a pressing character, and duty to a dependent family requiring his undivided attention, force him to abandon a task to which he has devoted the best years of his life, but which seems as far from accomplishment as at the start. He is, therefore, compelled, however unwillingly, to relinquish to others the elucidation of the Beale papers, not doubting that of the many who will give the subject attention, some one, through fortune or accident, will speedily solve their mystery and secure the prize which has eluded him.

"It can be readily imagined that this course was not determined upon all at once; regardless of the entreaties of his family and the persistent advice of his friend, who were formerly as sanguine as himself, he stubbornly continued his investigations, until absolute want stared him in the face and forced him to yield to their persuasions. Having now lost all hope of benefit from this source himself, he is not unwilling that others may receive it, and only hopes that the prize may fall to some poor, but honest man, who will use his discovery not solely for the promotion of his own enjoyment, but for the welfare of others.

"Until the writer lost all hope of ultimate success, he toiled faithfully at his work; unlike any other pursuit with practical and natural results, a charm attended it, independent of the ultimate benefit he expected, and the possibility of success lent an interest and excitement to the work not to be resisted.

"It would be difficult to portray the delight he experienced when accident revealed to him the explanation of the paper marked "2." Unmeaning, as this had hitherto been, it was now fully explained, and no difficulty was apprehended in mastering the others; but this accident, affording so much pleasure at the time, was a most unfortunate one for him, as it induced him to neglect family, friends, and all legitimate pursuits for what has proved, so far, the veriest illusion.

"It will be seen by a perusal of Mr. Beale's letter to Mr. Morriss that he promised, under certain contingences, such as failure to see or communicate with him in a given time, to furnishing a key by which the papers would be fully explained.

"As the failure to do either actually occurred, and the promised explanation has never been received, it may possibly remain in the hands of some relative or friend of Beale's, or some other person engaged in the enterprise with him. That they would attach no importance to a seemingly unintelligible writing seems quite natural; but their attention being called to them by the publication of this narrative, may result in eventually bringing to light the missing paper.

"Mr. Beale, who deposited with Mr. Morriss the papers which form the subject of this history, is described as being a gentleman well educated, evidently of good family, and with popular manners. What motives could have influenced him and so many others to risk their health and their lives in such an undertaking, except the natural love of daring adventure, with its consequent excitement, we can only conjecture.

"We may suppose, and indeed we have his word for so doing, that they were infatuated with the dangers, and with the wild and roving character of their lives, the charms of which lured them farther and farther from civilization, until their lives were sacrificed to their temerity. This was the opinion of Mr. Morriss, and in this way only can we account for the fact that the treasure for which they sacrificed so much, constituting almost fabulous wealth, lies abandoned and unclaimed for more than half a century.

"Should any of my readers be more fortunate than myself in discovering its place of concealment, I shall not only rejoice with them, but feel that I have at least accomplished something in contributing to the happiness of others.

"THE LATE ROBERT MORRISS

"Robert Morriss, the custodian of the Beale papers, was born in 1778, in the State of Maryland, but removed at an early age, with his family, to Loudoun county, Va., where, in 1803, he married Miss Sarah Mitchell, a fine looking and accomplished young lady of that county.

"In obtaining such a wife Mr. Morriss was peculiarly fortunate, as her subsequent career fully demonstrated. As a wife she was without reproach, as a generous and sympathizing woman she was without an equal; the poor will long remember her charities, and lament the friend they have lost.

"Shortly after his removal to Lynchburg, Mr. Morriss engaged in the mercantile business, and shortly thereafter he became a purchaser and shipper of tobacco to an extent hitherto unknown in this section. In these pursuits he was eminently successful for several years, and speedily accumulated a comfortable independence.

"It was during this period of his success that he erected the first brick building of which the town could boast, and which still stands on Main street, a monument to his enterprise. His private residence, the house now owned and occupied by Max Guggenheimer, Esq., at the head of Main street, I think he also built. There the most unbounded hospitality reigned, and every facility for enjoyment was furnished. The elite of the town assembled there more frequently than elsewhere, and there are now living some whose most pleasant recollections are associated with that period.

"The happiness of Mr. Morriss, however, was of short duration, and reverses came when they were least expected. Heavy purchases of tobacco, at ruinous figures, in anticipation of an upward market, which visions were never realized, swept from him in a moment the savings of years, and left him nothing save his honor and the sincere sympathy of the community with which to begin the battle anew.

"It was at this time that Mrs. Morriss exhibited the loveliest traits of her character. Seemingly unmindful of her condition, with a smiling face and cheering words, she so encouraged her husband that he became almost reconciled to his fate.

"Thrown thus upon his own resources, by the advice of his wife, he leased for a term of years the Washington Hotel, known now as the Arlington, on Church street, and commenced the business of hotel keeping. His kind disposition, strict probity, excellent management, and well ordered household, soon rendered him famous as a host, and his reputation extended even to other States. His was the house par excellence of the town, and no fashionable assemblages met at any other.

"Finding, in a few years, that his experiment was successful and his business remunerative, he removed to the Franklin Hotel, now the Norvell House, the largest and best arranged in the city. This house he conducted for many years, enjoying the friendship and countenance of the first men of the country. Amongst his guests and devoted personal friends Jackson, Clay, Coles, Witcher, Chief Justice

Marshall, and a host of others scarcely less distinguished, might be enumerated.

"But it was not the wealthy and distinguished alone who appreciated Mr. Morriss; the poor and lowly had blessings for the man who sympathized with their misfortunes, and was ever ready to relieve their distress. Many poor but worthy families, whose descendants are now in our midst, can remember the fact that his table supplied their daily food, not for days and weeks only, but for months at a time; and as a farther instance of his forbearance and unparalleled generosity, there are now living those who will testify to the fact that he permitted a boarder in no way connected with him, to remain in his house for more than twenty years, and until he died, without ever receiving the slightest renumeration, and that he was never made to feel otherwise than as a favored guest.

"In manner Mr. Morriss was courteous and gentle; but when occasion demanded, could be stern and determined, too; he was emphatically the master of his house, and from his decision there was no appeal. As an "old Virginia gentleman," he was sans peur et sans reproache, and to a remarkable extent possessed the confidence and affection of his friends.

"After a checquered and eventful life of more than eighty years, passed mostly in business, which brought him in contact with all classes of people, he died, lamented by all, and leaving not an enemy behind. His death, which occurred in 1863, was just two years subsequent to that of his wife. It can be truly said that no persons ever lived in a community for such a length of time who accomplished more good during their lives, or whose death was more universally regretted.

"It was the unblemished character of the man, and the universal confidence reposed in him, that induced Beale to entrust him with his secret, and in certain contingencies select him for a most important trust; that his confidence was not misplaced, every one remembering Mr. Morriss will acknowledge.

"It was in 1862, the second year of the Confederate war, that Mr. Morriss first intimated the possession of a secret that was destined to make some persons wealthy. At first he was not very communicative, nor did I press him to reveal what he seemed to speak of with reluctance; in a few weeks, however, his mind seemed changed, and he voluntarily proffered his confidence.

"Inviting me to his room, with no one to interrupt us, he gave me an outline of the matter, which soon enlisted my interest and created an intense longing to learn more. About this time, however, affairs of importance required my presence in Richmond, and prevented further communication between us until after my return, when I found him ready to resume the interesting subject. A private interview was soon arranged, and, after several preliminaries had been complied with, the papers upon which this history is based were delivered into my possession.

"The reasons which influenced him in selecting me for the trust, he gave, and were in substance as follows: First: Friendship for myself and family, whom he would benefit if he could. Second: The knowledge that I was young and in circumstances to afford leisure for the task imposed; and finally, a confidence that I would regard his instructions, and carry out his wishes regarding his charge. These, and perhaps others, he gave during our frequent conversations upon the subject, and doubtless believed he was conferring a favor which would redound greatly to my advantage. That is has proved otherwise is a misfortune to me, but no fault of his.

"The conditions alluded to above were that I should devote as much time as was practicable to the papers he had given me; master, if possible, their contents, and if successful in deciphering their meaning and eventually finding the treasure, to appropriate one-half of his portion as a remuneration for my services; the other half to be distributed to certain relatives and connexions of his own, whose names he gave me; the remainder to be held by me in trust for the benefit of such claimants as might at any time appear, and be able to authenticate their claims. This latter amount, to be left intact, subject to such demands, for the space of twenty years, when, if still unclaimed, it should revert to myself or my heirs, as a legacy from himself.

"As there was nothing objectionable in this, the required promise was given, and the box and the contents were placed in my possession.

"When the writer recalls his anxious hours, his midnight vigils, his toils, his hopes and disappointments, all consequent upon this promise, he can only conclude that the legacy of Mr. Morriss was not as he designed it - a blessing in disguise.

"Having assumed the responsibilities and consented to the requirements of Mr. Morriss, I determined to devote as much time to the accomplishment of the task as could be consistently spared from other duties. With this purpose in view, I requested from Mr. Morriss a statement of every particular connected with the affair, or having the slightest bearing upon it, together with such views and opinions of his own as might ultimately benefit me in my researches. In reply, he gave me the following, which I reduced to writing and filed with the papers for future reference:

"It was in the month of January, 1820, while keeping the Washington Hotel, that I first saw and became acquainted with Beale. In company with two others, he came to my house seeking entertainment for himself and friends. Being assured of a comfortable provision for themselves and their horses, Beale stated his intention of remaining for the winter, should nothing occur to alter his plans, but that the gentlemen accompanying him would leave in a few days for Richmond, near which place they resided, and that they were anxious to reach their homes, from which they had long been absent.

"They all appeared to be gentlemen, well born, and well educated, with refined and courteous manners and with a free and independent air, which rendered then peculiarly attractive. After remaining a week or ten days, the two left, after expressions of satisfaction with their visit. Beale, who remained, soon became a favored and popular guest; his social disposition and friendly demeanor rendered him extremely popular with every one, particularly the ladies, and a pleasant and friendly intercourse was quickly established between them.

"In person, he was about six feet in height, with jet black eyes and hair of the same color, worn longer than was the style at that time. His form was symmetrical, and gave evidence of unusual strength and activity; but his distinguishing feature was a dark and swarthy complexion, as if much exposure to the sun and weather had thoroughly tanned and discolored him.

"This, however, did not detract from his appearance; and I thought him the handsomest man I had ever seen. Altogether, he was a model of manly beauty, favored by the ladies and envied by men. To the first he was reverentially tender and polite; to the latter, affable and courteous, when they kept within bounds, but, if they were supercilious or presuming, the lion was aroused, and woe to the man who offended him. Instances of this character occurred more than once while he was my guest, and always resulted in his demanding and receiving an apology. His character soon became universally known, and he was no longer troubled by impertinence.

"Such a man was Thomas J. Beale, as he appeared in 1820, and in his subsequent visit to my house. He registered simply from Virginia, but I am of the impression he was from some western portion of the State. Curiously enough, he never adverted to his family or to his antecedents, nor did

I question him concerning them, as I would have done had I dreamed of the interest that in the future would attach to his name.

"Mr. Beale remained with me until about the latter end of the following March, when he left, with the same friends who first accompanied him to my house, and who had returned some days before.

"After this I heard nothing from him until January, 1822, when he once more made his appearance, the same genial and popular gentleman as before, but, if possible, darker and swarthier than ever. His welcome was a genuine one, as all were delighted to see him.

"In the spring, at about the same time, he again left, but before doing so, handed me this box, as he said, contained papers of value and importance; and which he desired to leave in my charge until called for hereafter. Of course, I did not decline to receive them, but little imagined their importance until his letter from St. Louis was received. This letter I carefully preserved, and it will be given with these papers.

"The box was of iron, carefully locked, and of such weight as to render it a safe depository for articles of value. I placed it in a safe and secure place, where it could not be disturbed until such time as it should be demanded by its owner.

"The letter alluded to above was the last communication I ever received from Beale, and I never saw him again. I can only suppose that he was killed by Indians, afar from his home, though nothing was heard of his death. His companions, too, must all have shared his fate, as no one has ever demanded the box or claimed his effects.

"The box was left in my hands in the Spring of 1822, and by authority of his letter, I should have examined its contents in 1832, ten years thereafter, having heard nothing from Beale in the meantime; but it was not until 1845, some twenty-three years after it came into my possession, that I decided upon opening it. During that year I had the lock broken, and with the exception of the two letters addressed to myself, and some old receipts, found only some unintelligible papers, covered with figures, and totally incomprehensible to me.

"According to his letter, these papers convey all the information necessary to find the treasure he has concealed, and upon you devolves the responsibility of recovering it. Should you succeed you will be amply compensated for your work, and others near and dear to me will likewise be benefitted. The end is worth all your exertions, and I have every hope that success will reward your efforts."

"Such, in substance, was the statement of Mr. Morriss in answer to the various interrogations propounded to him; and finding that I could elicit no further information, I resolved to do the best I could with the limited means at my disposal.

"I commenced by reading over and over again the letters to Mr. Morriss, endeavoring to impress each syllable they contained on my memory, and to extract from them, if possible, some meaning or allusion that might give, perhaps, a faint or barely perceptible hint as a guide; no such clue, however, could I find, and where or how to commence was a problem I found most difficult to solve.

"To systematize a plan for my work I arranged the papers in the order of their length, and numbered them, designing to commence with the first, and devote my whole attention to that until I had either unravelled its meaning or was convinced of its impossibility - afterwards to take up the others and proceed as before.

"All of this I did in the course of time, but failed so completely that my hopes of solving the mystery were well nigh abandoned. My thoughts, however were constantly upon it, and the figures contained in each paper, in their regular order, were fixed in my memory. My impression was that each figure represented a letter, but as the numbers so greatly exceeded the letters of the alphabet, that many different numbers represented the same letter.

"With this idea, a test was made of every book I could procure, by numbering its letters and comparing the numbers with those of the manuscript; all to no purpose, however, until the Declaration of Independence afforded the clue to one of the papers, and revived all my hopes.

"To enable my readers to better understand the explanation of this paper, the Declaration of Independence is given herewith, and will be of interest to those designing to follow up my investigations.

"When I first made this discovery, I thought I had the key to the whole, but soon ascertained that further work was necessary before my task was completed. The encouragement afforded, however, by this discovery enabled me to proceed, and I have persisted in my labors to the present time. Now, as I have already said, I am forced by circumstances to devote my time to other pursuits, and to abandon hopes which were destined never to be realized.

"The following is the letter addressed to Mr. Morriss by Beale, and dated St. Louis, May, 1822, and was the latest communication ever received from him:

"St. Louis, Mo., May 9, 1822.

Robt. Morris, Esq.:

My Esteemed Friend:

Ever since leaving my comfortable quarters at your house I have been journeying to this place, and only succeeded in reaching it yesterday. I have had altogether a pleasant time, the weather being fine and the atmosphere bracing. I shall remain here a week or ten days longer, then "ho" for the plains, to hunt the buffalo and encounter the savage grizzlies. How long I may be absent I cannot now determine, certainly no less than two years, perhaps longer.

With regard to the box left in your charge, I have a few words to say, and, if you will permit me, give you some instructions concerning it. It contains papers vitally affecting the fortunes of myself and many others engaged in business with me, and in the event of my death, its loss might be irreparable. You will, therefore, see the necessity of guarding it with vigilance and care to prevent so great a catastrophe. It also contains some letters addressed to yourself, and which will be necessary to enlighten you concerning the business in which we are engaged. Should none of us ever return you will please preserve carefully the box for the period of ten years from the date of this letter, and if I, or no one with authority from me during that time demands its restoration, you will open it, which can be done by removing the lock.

You will find, in addition to the papers addressed to you, other papers which will be unintelligible without the aid of a key to assist you. Such a key I have left in the hands of a friend in this place, sealed, addressed to yourself, and endorsed not to be delivered until June, 1832. By means of this you will understand fully all you will be required to do.

I know you will cheerfully comply with my request, thus adding to the many obligations under which you have already placed me. In the meantime, should death or sickness happen to you, to which all are liable, please select from among your friends some one worthy, and to him hand this letter, and to him delegate your authority.

I have been thus particular in my instructions, in consequence of the somewhat perilous enterprise in which we are engaged, but trust we shall meet long ere the time expires, and so save you this trouble. Be the result what it may, however, the game is worth the candle, and we will play it to the end.

With kindest wishes for your most excellent wife, compliments to the ladies, a good word to enquiring friends, if there be any, and assurances of my highest esteem for yourself, I remain as ever,

Your sincere friend,

Thos. Jeff^n. Beale.

"After the reception of this letter, Mr. Morriss states that he was particularly careful to see the box securely placed where it could remain in absolute safety, so long as the exigencies of the case might require; the letter, too, he was equally careful to preserve for future use, should it be needed.

"Having done all that was required of him, Mr. Morriss could only await Beale's return, or some communication from him. In either case, he was disappointed.

"During this period rumors of Indian outrages and massacres were current, but no mention of Beale's name ever occurred. What became of him and his companions is left entirely to conjecture. Whether he was slain by Indians, or killed by the savage animals of the Rocky Mountains, or whether exposure, and perhaps privation, did its work can never be told. One thing at least is certain, that of the young and gallant band, whose buoyant spirits led them to seek such a life, and to forsake the comforts of home, with all its enjoyments, for the dangers and privations they must necessarily encounter, not a survivor remains.

"Though Mr. Morriss was aware of the contents of the box in 1845, it was not until 1862, forty years after he received it, that he thought proper to mention its existence, and to myself alone did he then divulge it. He had become long since satisfied that the parties were no longer living, but his delicacy of feeling prevented his assuming as a fact a matter so pregnant with consequences. He frequently decided upon doing so, and as often delayed it for another time; and when at last he did speak of the matter it was with seeming reluctance, and as if he felt he was committing a wrong. But the story once told, he evinced up to the time of his death the greatest interest in my success, and in frequent interviews always encouraged me to proceed.

"It is now more than twenty years since these papers came into my hands, and, with the exception of one of them, they are still as incomprehensible as ever. Much time was devoted to this one, and those who engage in the matter will be saved what has been consumed upon it by myself.

"Before giving the papers to the public, I would say a word to those who may take an interest in them, and give them a little advice, acquired by bitter experience. It is, to devote only such time as can be spared from your legitimate business to the task, and if you can spare no time, let the matter alone. Should you disregard my advice, do not hold me responsible that the poverty you have courted is more easily found than accomplishment of your wishes, and I would avoid the sight of another reduced to my condition.

"Nor is it necessary to devote the time that I did to this matter, as accident alone, without the promised key, will ever develop the mystery. If revealed by accident, a few hours devoted to the subject may accomplish results which were denied to years of patient toil. Again, never, as I have done, sacrifice your own and your family's interests to what may prove an illusion; but, as I have already said, when your day's work is done, and you are comfortably seated by your good fire, a short time devoted to the subject can injure no one, and may bring its reward.

"By pursuing this policy, your interests will not suffer, your family will be cared for, and your thoughts will not be absorbed to the exclusion of other important affairs. With this admonition, I submit to my readers the papers upon which this narrative is founded.

"The first in order is the letter from Beale to Mr. Morriss, which will give the reader a clearer conception of all the facts connected with the case, and enable him to understand as fully as I myself do, the present status of the affair. The letter is as follows:

Lynchburg, January 4th, 1822.

My Dear Friend Morriss:

You will, doubtless, be surprised when you discover, from a perusal of this letter, the importance of the trust confided to you, and the confidence reposed in your honor, by parties whom you have never seen, and whose names even you have never heard. The reasons are simple and easily told; it was imperative upon us that some one here should be selected to carry out our wishes in case of accident to ourselves, and your reputation as a man of the sternest integrity, unblemished honor, and business capacity, influenced them to select you in place of others better known, but perhaps, not so reliable as yourself.

It was with this design that I first visited your house, two years since, that I might judge by personal observation if your reputation was merited. To enable me better to do so, I remained with you more than three months, and until I was fully satisfied as to your character. This visit was made by the request of my associates, and you can judge from their action whether my report was a favorable one.

I will now give you some idea of the enterprise in which we are engaged, and the duties which will be required of you in connection therewith; first assuring you, however, that your compensation for the trouble will be ample, as you have been unanimously made one or our association, and as such are entitled to share equally with the others.

Some five years since I, in connection with several friends, who, like myself, were fond of adventure, and if mixed with a little danger all the more acceptable, determined to visit the great Western plains and enjoy ourselves in hunting buffalo, grizzly bears, and such other game as the country would afford. This, at that time, was our sole object, and we at once proceeded to put it in execution.

On account of Indians and other dangers incident to such an undertaking, we determined to raise a party of not less than thirty individuals, of good character and standing, who would be pleasant companions, and financially able to encounter the expense. With this object in view, each one of us suggested the matter to his several friends and acquaintances, and in a few weeks the requisite number had signed the conditions, and were admitted as members of the party. Some few refused to join with us, being, doubtless, deterred by the dangers, but such men we did not want, and were glad of their refusal.

The company being formed, we forthwith commenced our preparations, and, early in April, 1817, left old Virginia for St. Louis, Mo., where we expected to purchase the necessary outfits, procure a guide and two or three servants, and obtain such information and advice as might be beneficial hereafter. All was done as intended, and we left St. Louis the 19th of May, to be absent two years, our objective point being Santa Fe, which we intended to reach in the ensuing Fall, and there establish ourselves in winter quarters.

After leaving St. Louis we were advised by our guide to form a regular military organization, with a captain, to be selected by the members, to whom should be given sole authority to manage our affairs, and, in cases of necessity, ensure united action. This was agreed to, and each member of the party bound himself by a solemn obligation to obey at all times, the orders of their captain, or, in the event of refusal, to leave the company at once.

This arrangement was to remain in force for two years, or for the period of our expected absence. Tyranny, partiality, incompetency, or other improper conduct on the part of the captain, was to be punished by deposing him from his office, if a majority of the company desired his dismissal. All this being arranged, and a set of laws framed, by which the conduct of the members was to be regulated, the election was held, and resulted in choosing me as their leader.

It is not my purpose now to give you details of our wanderings, or of the pleasures or dangers we encountered. All this I will reserve until we meet again, when it will be a pleasure to recall incidents that will always be fresh in my memory.

About the first of December we reached our destination, Santa Fe, and prepared for a long and welcome rest from the fatigues of our journey. Nothing of interest occurred during the winter, and of this little Mexican town we soon became heartily tired. We longed for the advent of weather which would enable us to resume our wanderings and our exhilerating pursuits.

Early in March some of the party, to vary the monotony of their lives, determined upon a short excursion, for the purpose of hunting and examining the country around us. They expected to be only a few days absent, but days passed into weeks, and weeks into a month or more before we had any tidings of the party.

We had become exceedingly uneasy, and were preparing to send out scouts to trace them, if possible, when two of the party arrived, and gave an explanation of their absence. It appears that when the left Santa Fe they pursued a northerly course for some days, being successful in finding an abundance of game, which they secured, and were on the eve of returning when they discovered on their left an immense herd of buffaloes, heading for a valley just perceptible in the distance. They determined to follow them, and secure as many as possible. Keeping well together, they followed their trail for two weeks or more, securing many and stampeding the rest.

One day, while following them, the party encamped in a small ravine, some 250 or 300 miles to the north of Santa Fe, and with their horses tethered, were preparing their evening meal, when one of the men discovered in a cleft of the rocks something that had the appearance of gold. Upon showing it to the others it was pronounced to be gold, and much excitement was the natural consequence. Messengers were at once dispatched to inform me of the facts, and request my presence with the rest of the party, and with supplies for an indefinite time.

All the pleasures and temptations which had lured them to the plains were now forgotten, and visions of boundless wealth and future grandeur were the only ideas entertained.

Upon reaching the locality I found all as it had been represented, and the excitement intense. Every one was diligently at work with such tools and appliances as they had improvised, and quite a little pile had already accumulated. Though all were at work, there was nothing like order or method in their plans, and my first efforts were to systematize our operations, and reduce everything to order.

With this object, an agreement was entered into to work in common as joint partners, the accumulations of each one to be placed in a common receptacle, and each be entitled to an equal share, whenever he chose to withdraw it - the whole to remain under my charge until some other disposition of it was agreed upon. Under this arrangement the work progressed favorable for eighteen months or more, and a great deal of gold had accumulated in my hands as well as silver, which had likewise been found. Everything necessary for our purposes and for the prosecution of the work had been obtained from Santa Fe, and no trouble was experienced in procuring assistance from the Indians in our labors.

Matters went on thus until the summer of 1819, when the question of transferring our wealth to some secure place was frequently discussed. It was not considered advisable to retain so large an amount in so wild and dangerous a locality, where its very possession might endanger our lives; and to conceal it here would avail nothing, as we might at any time be forced to reveal its place of concealment.

We were in a dilemma. Some advised one plan, some another. One recommended Santa Fe as the safest place to deposit it, while others objected, and advocated its shipment at once to the States, where it was ultimately bound to go, and where alone it would be safe. The idea seemed to prevail, and it was doubtless correct, that when outside parties ascertained, as they would do, that we kept nothing on hand to tempt their cupidity, our lives would be more secure than at present.

It was finally decided that is should be sent to Virginia under my charge, and securely buried in a cave near Buford's tavern, in the county of Bedford, which all of us had visited, and which was considered a perfectly safe depository. This was acceptable to all, and I at once made preparations for my departure. The whole party were to accompany me for the first five hundred miles, when all but ten would return, these latter to remain with me to the end of the journey. All was carried out as arranged, and I arrived safely with my charge.

Stopping at Buford's, where we remained for a month, under pretense of hunting etc. we visited the cave, and found it unfit for our purpose. It was too frequently visited by the neighboring farmers, who used it as a receptacle for their sweet potatoes and other vegetables. We soon selected a better place, and to this the treasure was safely transferred.

Before leaving my companions on the plains it was suggested that, in case of an accident to ourselves, the treasure so concealed would be lost to their relatives, without some provision against such a contingency. I was, therefore instructed to select some perfectly reliable person, if such an one could be found, who should, in the event of his proving acceptable to the party, be confided in to carry out their wishes in regard to their respective shares, and upon my return report whether I had found such a person. It was in accordance with these instructions that I visited you, made your acquaintance, was satisfied that you would suit us, and so reported.

On my return I found the work still progressing favorably, and, by making large accessions to our force of laborers, I was ready to return last Fall with an increased supply of metal, which came through safely and was deposited with the other. It was at this time I handed you the box, not disclosing the nature of its contents, but asking you to keep it safely till called for. I intend writing you, however, from St. Louis, and impress upon you its importance still more forcibly.

The papers enclosed herewith will be unintelligible without the key, which will reach you in time, and will be found merely to state the contents of our depository, with its exact location, and a list of the names of our party, with their places of residence, etc.

I thought at first to give you their names in this letter, but reflecting that some one may read the letter, and thus be enabled to impose upon you by personating some member of the party, have decided the present plan is best.

You will be aware from what I have written, that we are engaged in a perilous enterprise - one which promises glorious results if successful - but dangers intervene, and of the end no one can tell. We can only hope for the best, and persevere until our work is accomplished, and the sum secured for which we are striving.

As ten years must elapse before you will see this letter, you may well conclude by that time that the worst has happened, and that none of us are to be numbered with the living. In such an event, you will please visit the place of deposit and secure its contents, which you will divide into thirty-one equal parts; one of these parts you are to retain as your own, freely given to you for your services. The other shares to be distributed to the parties named in the accompanying paper. These legacies, so unexpectedly received, will at least serve to recall names that may still be cherished, though partially forgotten.

In conclusion, my dear friend, I beg that you will not allow any false or idle punctillio to prevent your receiving and appropriating the portion assigned to yourself. It is a gift not from myself alone, but from each and every member of our party, and will not be out of proportion to the services required of you.

I trust, my dear Mr. Morriss, that we may meet many times in the future, but if the Fates forbid, with my last communication I would assure you of the entire respect and confidence of

Your friend,

s n
Tho . Jeff . Beale.

"The second letter in the box is as follows:

Lynchburg, Va., January 5th, 1822.

Dear Mr. Morriss. –

You will find in one of the papers, written in cipher, the names of all my associates, who are each entitled to an equal part of our treasure, and opposite to the names of each one will be found the names and residences of the relatives and others, to whom they devise their respective portions.

From this you will be enabled to carry out the wishes of all by distributing the portion of each to the parties designated. This will not be difficult, as their residences are given, and they can easily be found.

T.J.B.

"The two letters given above were all the box contained that were intelligible. The others, consisted of papers closely covered with figures, which were, of course, unmeaning until they could be deciphered. To do this was the task to which I now devoted myself, and with but partial success, that is, as to deciphering paper marked "No. 2", to be described later on.

The three ciphers are given below, the one marked "No. 1" describing the exact locality of the vault where the treasure is buried the one marked "No. 2" stating the contents of the vault; and the paper marked "No. 3" stating the names and addresses of the persons involved:

"No. 1"

71, 194, 38, 1701, 89, 76, 11, 83, 1629, 48, 94, 63, 132, 16, 111, 95, 84, 341, 975, 14, 40, 64, 27, 81, 139, 213, 63, 90, 1120, 8, 15, 3, 126, 2018, 40, 74, 758, 485, 604, 230, 436, 664, 582, 150, 251, 284, 308, 231, 124, 211, 486, 225, 401, 370, 11, 101, 305, 139, 189, 17, 33, 88, 208, 193, 145, 1, 94, 73, 416, 918, 263, 28, 500, 538, 356, 117, 136, 219, 27, 176, 130, 10, 460, 25, 485, 18, 436, 65, 84, 200, 283, 118, 320, 138, 36, 416, 280, 15, 71, 224, 961, 44, 16, 401, 39, 88, 61, 304, 12, 21, 24, 283, 134, 92, 63, 246, 486, 682, 7, 219, 184, 360, 780, 18, 64, 463, 474, 131, 160, 79, 73, 440, 95, 18, 64, 581, 34, 69, 128, 367, 460, 17, 81, 12, 103, 820, 62, 116, 97, 103, 862, 70, 60, 1317, 471, 540, 208, 121, 890, 346, 36, 150, 59, 568, 614, 13, 120, 63, 219, 812, 2160, 1780, 99, 35, 18, 21, 136, 872, 15, 28, 170, 88, 4, 30, 44, 112, 18, 147, 436, 195, 320, 37, 122, 113, 6, 140, 8, 120, 305, 42, 58, 461, 44, 106, 301, 13, 408, 680, 93, 86, 116, 530, 82, 568, 9, 102, 38, 416, 89, 71, 216, 728, 965, 818, 2, 38, 121, 195, 14, 326, 148, 234, 18, 55, 131, 234, 361, 824, 5, 81, 623, 48, 961, 19, 26, 33, 10, 1101, 365, 92, 88, 181, 275, 346, 201, 206, 86, 36, 219, 324, 829, 840, 64, 326, 19, 48, 122, 85, 216, 284, 919, 861, 326, 985, 233, 64, 68, 232, 431, 960, 50, 29, 81, 216, 321, 603, 14, 612, 81, 360, 36, 51, 62, 194, 78, 60, 200, 314, 676, 112, 4, 28, 18, 61, 136, 247, 819, 921, 1060, 464, 895, 10, 6, 66, 119, 38, 41, 49, 602, 423, 962, 302, 294, 875, 78, 14, 23, 111, 109, 62, 31, 501, 823, 216, 280, 34, 24, 150, 1000, 162, 286, 19, 21, 17, 340, 19, 242, 31, 86, 234, 140, 607, 115, 33, 191, 67, 104, 86, 52, 88, 16, 80, 121, 67, 95, 122, 216, 548, 96, 11, 201, 77, 364, 218, 65, 667, 890, 236, 154, 211, 10, 98, 34, 119, 56, 216, 119, 71, 218, 1164, 1496, 1817, 51, 39, 210, 36, 3, 19, 540, 232, 22, 141, 617, 84, 290, 80, 46, 207, 411, 150, 29, 38, 46, 172, 85, 194, 39, 261, 543, 897, 624, 18, 212, 416, 127, 931, 19, 4, 63, 96, 12, 101, 418, 16, 140, 230, 460, 538, 19, 27, 88, 612, 1431, 90, 716, 275, 74, 83, 11, 426, 89, 72, 84, 1300, 1706, 814, 221, 132, 40, 102, 34, 868, 975, 1101, 84, 16, 79, 23, 16, 81, 122, 324,

403, 912, 227, 936, 447, 55, 86, 34, 43, 212, 107, 96, 314, 264, 1065, 323, 428, 601, 203, 124, 95, 216, 814, 2906, 654, 820, 2, 301, 112, 176, 213, 71, 87, 96, 202, 35, 10, 2, 41, 17, 84, 221, 736, 820, 214, 11, 60, 760

"No. 2"

115, 73, 24, 807, 37, 52, 49, 17, 31, 62, 647, 22, 7, 15, 140, 47, 29, 107, 79, 84, 56, 239, 10, 26, 811, 5, 196, 308, 85, 52, 160, 136, 59, 211, 36, 9, 46, 316, 554, 122, 106, 95, 53, 58, 2, 42, 7, 35, 122, 53, 31, 82, 77, 250, 196, 56, 96, 118, 71, 140, 287, 28, 353, 37, 1005, 65, 147, 807, 24, 3, 8, 12, 47, 43, 59, 807, 45, 316, 101, 41, 78, 154, 1005, 122, 138, 191, 16, 77, 49, 102, 57, 72, 34, 73, 85, 35, 371, 59, 196, 81, 92, 191, 106, 273, 60, 394, 620, 270, 220, 106, 388, 287, 63, 3, 6, 191, 122, 43, 234, 400, 106, 290, 314, 47, 48, 81, 96, 26, 115, 92, 158, 191, 110, 77, 85, 197, 46, 10, 113, 140, 353, 48, 120, 106, 2, 607, 61, 420, 811, 29, 125, 14, 20, 37, 105, 28, 248, 16, 159, 7, 35, 19, 301, 125, 110, 486, 287, 98, 117, 511, 62, 51, 220, 37, 113, 140, 807, 138, 540, 8, 44, 287, 388, 117, 18, 79, 344, 34, 20, 59, 511, 548, 107, 603, 220, 7, 66, 154, 41, 20, 50, 6, 575, 122, 154, 248, 110, 61, 52, 33, 30, 5, 38, 8, 14, 84, 57, 540, 217, 115, 71, 29, 84, 63, 43, 131, 29, 138, 47, 73, 239, 540, 52, 53, 79, 118, 51, 44, 63, 196, 12, 239, 112, 3, 49, 79, 353, 105, 56, 371, 557, 211, 505, 125, 360, 133, 143, 101, 15, 284, 540, 252, 14, 205, 140, 344, 26, 811, 138, 115, 48, 73, 34, 205, 316, 607, 63, 220, 7, 52, 150, 44, 52, 16, 40, 37, 158, 807, 37, 121, 12, 95, 10, 15, 35, 12, 131, 62, 115, 102, 807, 49, 53, 135, 138, 30, 31, 62, 67, 41, 85, 63, 10, 106, 807, 138, 8, 113, 20, 32, 33, 37, 353, 287, 140, 47, 85, 50, 37, 49, 47, 64, 6, 7, 71, 33, 4, 43, 47, 63, 1, 27, 600, 208, 230, 15, 191, 246, 85, 94, 511, 2, 270, 20, 39, 7, 33, 44, 22, 40, 7, 10, 3, 811, 106, 44, 486, 230, 353, 211, 200, 31, 10, 38, 140, 297, 61, 603, 320, 302, 666, 287, 2, 44, 33, 32, 511, 548, 10, 6, 250, 557, 246, 53, 37, 52, 83, 47, 320, 38, 33, 807, 7, 44, 30, 31, 250, 10, 15, 35, 106, 160, 113, 31, 102, 406, 230, 540, 320, 29, 66, 33, 101, 807, 138, 301, 316, 353, 320, 220, 37, 52, 28, 540, 320, 33, 8, 48, 107, 50, 811, 7, 2, 113, 73, 16, 125, 11, 110, 67, 102, 807, 33, 59, 81, 158, 38, 43, 581, 138, 19, 85, 400, 38, 43, 77, 14, 27, 8, 47, 138, 63, 140, 44, 35, 22, 177, 106, 250, 314, 217, 2, 10, 7, 1005, 4, 20, 25, 44, 48, 7, 26, 46, 110, 230, 807, 191,

34, 112, 147, 44, 110, 121, 125, 96, 41, 51, 50, 140, 56, 47, 152, 540, 63, 807, 28, 42, 250, 138, 582, 98, 643, 32, 107, 140, 112, 26, 85, 138, 540, 53, 20, 125, 371, 38, 36, 10, 52, 118, 136, 102, 420, 150, 112, 71, 14, 20, 7, 24, 18, 12, 807, 37, 67, 110, 62, 33, 21, 95, 220, 511, 102, 811, 30, 83, 84, 305, 620, 15, 2, 10, 8, 220, 106, 353, 105, 106, 60, 275, 72, 8, 50, 205, 185, 112, 125, 540, 65, 106, 807, 138, 96, 110, 16, 73, 33, 807, 150, 409, 400, 50, 154, 285, 96, 106, 316, 270, 205, 101, 811, 400, 8, 44, 37, 52, 40, 241, 34, 205, 38, 16, 46, 47, 85, 24, 44, 15, 64, 73, 138, 807, 85, 78, 110, 33, 420, 505, 53, 37, 38, 22, 31, 10, 110, 106, 101, 140, 15, 38, 3, 5, 44, 7, 98, 287, 135, 150, 96, 33, 84, 125, 807, 191, 96, 511, 118, 40, 370, 643, 466, 106, 41, 107, 603, 220, 275, 30, 150, 105, 49, 53, 287, 250, 208, 134, 7, 53, 12, 47, 85, 63, 138, 110, 21, 112, 140, 485, 486, 505, 14, 73, 84, 575, 1005, 150, 200, 16, 42, 5, 4, 25, 42, 8, 16, 811, 125, 160, 32, 205, 603, 807, 81, 96, 405, 41, 600, 136, 14, 20, 28, 26, 353, 302, 246, 8, 131, 160, 140, 84, 440, 42, 16, 811, 40, 67, 101, 102, 194, 138, 205, 51, 63, 241, 540, 122, 8, 10, 63, 140, 47, 48, 140, 288

"No. 3"

317, 8, 92, 73, 112, 89, 67, 318, 28, 96,107, 41, 631, 78, 146, 397, 118, 98, 114, 246, 348, 116, 74, 88, 12, 65, 32, 14, 81, 19, 76, 121, 216, 85, 33, 66, 15, 108, 68, 77, 43, 24, 122, 96, 117, 36, 211, 301, 15, 44, 11, 46, 89, 18, 136, 68, 317, 28, 90, 82, 304, 71, 43, 221, 198, 176, 310, 319, 81, 99, 264, 380, 56, 37, 319, 2, 44, 53, 28, 44, 75, 98, 102, 37, 85, 107, 117, 64, 88, 136, 48, 151, 99, 175, 89, 315, 326, 78, 96, 214, 218, 311, 43, 89, 51, 90, 75, 128, 96, 33, 28, 103, 84, 65, 26, 41, 246, 84, 270, 98, 116, 32, 59, 74, 66, 69, 240, 15, 8, 121, 20, 77, 89, 31, 11, 106, 81, 191, 224, 328, 18, 75, 52, 82, 117, 201, 39, 23, 217, 27, 21, 84, 35, 54, 109, 128, 49, 77, 88, 1, 81, 217, 64, 55, 83, 116, 251, 269, 311, 96, 54, 32, 120, 18, 132, 102, 219, 211, 84, 150, 219, 275, 312, 64, 10, 106, 87, 75, 47, 21, 29, 37, 81, 44, 18, 126, 115, 132, 160, 181, 203, 76, 81, 299, 314, 337, 351, 96, 11, 28, 97, 318, 238, 106, 24, 93, 3, 19, 17, 26, 60, 73, 88, 14, 126, 138, 234, 286, 297, 321, 365, 264, 19, 22, 84, 56, 107, 98, 123, 111, 214, 136, 7, 33, 45, 40, 13, 28, 46, 42, 107, 196, 227, 344, 198, 203, 247, 116, 19, 8, 212, 230, 31, 6, 328, 65, 48, 52, 59, 41, 122, 33, 117, 11, 18, 25, 71,

36, 45, 83, 76, 89, 92, 31, 65, 70, 83, 96, 27, 33, 44, 50, 61, 24, 112, 136, 149, 176, 180, 194, 143, 171, 205, 296, 87, 12, 44, 51, 89, 98, 34, 41, 208, 173, 66, 9, 35, 16, 95, 8, 113, 175, 90, 56, 203, 19, 177, 183, 206, 157, 200, 218, 260, 291, 305, 618, 951, 320, 18, 124, 78, 65, 19, 32, 124, 48, 53, 57, 84, 96, 207, 244, 66, 82, 119, 71, 11, 86, 77, 213, 54, 82, 316, 245, 303, 86, 97, 106, 212, 18, 37, 15, 81, 89, 16, 7, 81, 39, 96, 14, 43, 216, 118, 29, 55, 109, 136, 172, 213, 64, 8, 227, 304, 611, 221, 364, 819, 375, 128, 296, 1, 18, 53, 76, 10, 15, 23, 19, 71, 84, 120, 134, 66, 73, 89, 96, 230, 48, 77, 26, 101, 127, 936, 218, 439, 178, 171, 61, 226, 313, 215, 102, 18, 167, 262, 114, 218, 66, 59, 48, 27, 19, 13, 82, 48, 162, 119, 34, 127, 139, 34, 128, 129, 74, 63, 120, 11, 54, 61, 73, 92, 180, 66, 75, 101, 124, 265, 89, 96, 126, 274, 896, 917, 434, 461, 235, 890, 312, 413, 328, 381, 96, 105, 217, 66, 118, 22, 77, 64, 42, 12, 7, 55, 24, 83, 67, 97, 109, 121, 135, 181, 203, 219, 228, 256, 21, 34, 77, 319, 374, 382, 675, 684, 717, 864, 203, 4, 18, 92, 16, 63, 82, 22, 46, 55, 69, 74, 112, 134, 186, 175, 119, 213, 416, 312, 343, 264, 119, 186, 218, 343, 417, 845, 951, 124, 209, 49, 617, 856, 924, 936, 72, 19, 28, 11, 35, 42, 40, 66, 85, 94, 112, 65, 82, 115, 119, 236, 244, 186, 172, 112, 85, 6, 56, 38, 44, 85, 72, 32, 47, 63, 96, 124, 217, 314, 319, 221, 644, 817, 821, 934, 922, 416, 975, 10, 22, 18, 46, 137, 181, 101, 39, 86, 103, 116, 138, 164, 212, 218, 296, 815, 380, 412, 460, 495, 675, 820, 952

"The papers given above were all that were contained in the box, except two or three of an unimportant character, and having no connection whatever with the subject in hand. They were carefully copied, and as carefully compared with the originals, and no error is believed to exist.

"Complete in themselves, they are respectfully submitted to the public, with the hope that all that is dark in them may receive light, and that the treasure, amounting to more than three-quarters of a million, which has rested so long unproductive of good, in the hands of a proper person, may eventually accomplish its mission.

"To enable my readers to understand the paper "No.2", the only one I was ever able to decipher, I herewith give the Declaration of Independence, with the words numbered consecutively, by the assistance of which that paper's hidden meaning was made plain:

IN CONGRESS JULY 4, 1776.
A Declaration by the Representatives of the
UNITED STATES OF AMERICA
In General Congress Assembled

When(1) in(2) the(3) course(4) of(5) human(6) events(7) it(8) becomes(9) necessary(10) for(11) one(12) people(13) to(14) dissolve(15) the(16) political(17) bands(18) which(19) have(20) connected(21) them(22) with(23) another(24) and(25) to(26) assume(27) among(28) the(29) powers(30) of(31) the(32) earth(33) the(34) separate(35) and(36) equal(37) station(38) to(39) which(40) the(41) laws(42) of(43) nature(44) and(45) of(46) nature's(47) god(48) entitle(49) them(50) a(51) decent(52) respect(53) to(54) the(55) opinions(56) of(57) mankind(58) requires(59) that(60) they(61) should(62) declare(63) the(64) causes(65) which(66) impel(67) them(68) to(69) the(70) separation(71) we(72) hold(73) these(74) truths(75) to(76) be(77) self(78) evident(79) that(80) all(81) men(82) are(83) created(84) equal(85) that(86) they(87) are(88) endowed(89) by(90) their(91) creator(92) with(93) certain(94) unalienable(95) rights(96) that(97) among(98) these(99) are(100) life(101) liberty(102) and(103) the(104) pursuit(105) of(106) happiness(107) that(108) to(109) secure(110) these(111) rights(112) governments(113) are(114) instituted(115) among(116) men(117) deriving(118) their(119) just(120) powers(121) from(122) the(123) consent(124) of(125) the(126) governed(127) that(128) whenever(129) any(130) form(131) of(132) government(133) becomes(134) destructive(135) of(136) these(137) ends(138) it(139) is(140) the(141) right(142) of(143) the(144) people(145) to(146) alter(147) or(148) to(149) abolish(150) it(151) and(152) to(153) institute(154) new(155) government(156) laying(157) its(158) foundation(159) on(160) such(161) principles(162) and(163) organizing(164) its(165) powers(166) in(167) such(168) form(169) as(170) to(171) them(172) shall(173) seem(174) most(175) likely(176) to(177) effect(178) their(179) safety(180) and(181) happiness(182) prudence(183) indeed(184) will(185) dictate(186) that(187) governments(188) long(189) established(190) should(191) not(192) be(193) changed(194) for(195) light(196) and(197) transient(198) causes(199) and(200) accordingly(201) all(202) experience(203) hath(204) shown(205) that(206) mankind(207) are(208) more(209) disposed(210) to(211) suffer(212) while(213) evils(214) are(215) sufferable(216) than(217) to(218) right(219) themselves(220) by(221) abolishing(222) the(223) forms(224) to(225) which(226) they(227) are(228) accustomed(229) but(230) when(231) a(232) long(233) train(234) of(235) abuses(236) and(237) usurpations(238) pursuing(239) invariably(240) the(241) same(242) object(243) evinces(244) a(245) design(246) to(247) reduce(248) them(249) under(250) absolute(251) despotism(252) it(253) is(254) their(255) right(256) it(257) is(258) their(259) duty(260) to(261) throw(262) off(263) such(264) government(265) and(266) to(267) provide(268) new(269) guards(270) for(271) their(272) future(273) security(274) such(275) has(276) been(277) the(278) patient(279) sufferance(280) of(281) these(282) colonies(283) and(284) such(285) is(286) now(287) the(288) necessity(289) which(290) constrains(291) them(292) to(293) alter(294) their(295) former(296) systems(297) of(298) government(299) the(300) history(301) of(302) the(303) present(304) king(305) of(306) great(307) Britain(308) is(309) a(310) history(311) of(312) repeated(313) injuries(314) and(315) usurpations(316) all(317) having(318) in(319) direct(320) object(321) the(322) establishment(323) of(324) an(325) absolute(326) tyranny(327) over(328) these(329) states(330) to(331) prove(332) this(333) let(334) facts(335) be(336) submitted(337) to(338) a(339) candid(340) world(341) he(342) has(343) refused(344) his(345) assent(346) to(347) laws(348) the(349) most(350) wholesome(351) and(352) necessary(353) for(354) the(355) public(356) good(357) he(358) has(359) forbidden(360) his(361) governors(362) to(363) pass(364) laws(365) of(366) immediate(367) and(368) pressing(369) importance(370) unless(371) suspended(372) in(373) their(374) operation(375) till(376) his(377) assent(378) should(379) be(380) obtained(381) and(382) when(383) so(384) suspended(385) he(386) has(387) utterly(388) neglected(389) to(390) attend(391) to(392) them(393) he(394) has(395) refused(396) to(397) pass(398) other(399) laws(400) for(401) the(402) accommodation(403) of(404) large(405) districts(406) of(407) people(408) unless(409) those(410) people(411) would(412) relinquish(413) the(414) right(415) of(416) representation(417) in(418) the(419) legislature(420) a(421) right(422) inestimable(423) to(424) them(425) and(426) formidable(427) to(428) tyrants(429) only(430) he(431) has(432) called(433) together(434) legislative(435) bodies(436) at(437) places(438) unusual(439) uncomfortable(440) and(441) distant(442) from(443) the(444) depository(445) of(446) their(447) public(448) records(449) for(450) the(451) sole(452) purpose(453) of(454) fatiguing(455) them(456) into(457) compliance(458) with(459) his(460) measures(461) he(462) has(463) dissolved(464) representative(465) houses(466) repeatedly(467) for(468) opposing(469) with(470) manly(471) firmness(472) his(473) invasions(474) on(475) the(476) rights(477) of(478) the(479) people(480) he(481) has(482) refused(483) for(484) a(485) long(486) time(487) after(488) such(489) dissolutions(490) to(491) cause(492) others(493) to(494) be(495) elected(496) whereby(497) the(498) legislative(499) powers(500) incapable(501) of(502) annihilation(503) have(504) returned(505) to(506) the(507) people(508) at(509) large(510) for(511) their(512) exercise(513) the(514) state(515) remaining(516) in(517) the(518) meantime(519) exposed(520) to(521) all(522) the(523) dangers(524) of(525) invasion(526) from(527) without(528) and(529) convulsions(530) within(531) he(532) has(533) endeavored(534) to(535) prevent(536) the(537) population(538) of(539) these(540) states(541) for(542) that(543) purpose(544) obstructing(545) the(546) laws(547) for(548) naturalization(549) of(550) foreigners(551) refusing(552) to(553) pass(554) others(555) to(556) encourage(557) their(558) migration(559) hither(560) and(561) raising(562) the(563) conditions(564) of(565) new(566) appropriations(567) of(568) lands(569) he(570) has(571) obstructed(572) the(573) administration(574) of(575) justice(576) by(577) refusing(578) his(579) assent(580) to(581) laws(582) for(583) establishing(584) judiciary(585) powers(586) he(587) has(588) made(589) judges(590) dependent(591) on(592) his(593) will(594) alone(595) for(596) the(597) tenure(598) of(599) their(600) offices(601) and(602) the(603) amount(604) and(605) payment(606) of(607) their(608) salaries(609) he(610) has(611) erected(612) a(613) multitude(614) of(615) new(616) offices(617) and(618) sent(619) hither(620) swarms(621) of(622) officers(623) to(624) harass(625) our(626) people(627) and(628) eat(629) out(630) their(631) substance(632) he(633) has(634) kept(635) among(636) us(637) in(638) times(639) of(640) peace(641) standing(642) armies(643) without(644) the(645) consent(646) of(647) our(648) legislatures(649) he(650) has(651) affected(652) to(653) render(654) the(655) military(656) independent(657) of(658) and(659) superior(660) to(661) the(662) civil(663) power(664) he(665) has(666) combined(667) with(668) others(669) to(670) subject(671) us(672) to(673) a(674) jurisdiction(675) foreign(676) to(677) our(678) constitution(679) and(680) unacknowledged(681) by(682) our(683) laws(684) giving(685) his(686) assent(687) to(688) their(689) acts(690) of(691) pretended(692) legislation(693) for(694) quartering(695) large(696) bodies(697) of(698) armed(699) troops(700) among(701) us(702) for(703) protecting(704) them(705) by(706) a(707) mock(708) trial(709) from(710) punishment(711) for(712) any(713) murders(714) which(715) they(716) should(717) commit(718) on(719) the(720) inhabitants(721) of(722) these(723) states(724) for(725) cutting(726) off(727) our(728) trade(729) with(730) all(731) parts(732) of(733) the(734) world(735) for(736) imposing(737) taxes(738) on(739) us(740) without(741) our(742) consent(743) for(744) depriving(745) us(746) in(747) many(748) cases(749) of(750) the(751) benefits(752) of(753) trial(754) by(755) jury(756) for(757) transporting(758) us(759) beyond(760) seas(761) to(762) be(763) tried(764) for(765) pretended(766) offenses(767) for(768) abolishing(769) the(770) free(771) system(772) of(773) English(774) laws(775) in(776) a(777) neighboring(778) province(779) establishing(780) therein(781) an(782) arbitrary(783) government(784) and(785) enlarging(786) its(787) boundaries(788) so(789) as(790) to(791) render(792) it(793) at(794) once(795) an(796) example(797) and(798) fit(799) instrument(800) for(801) introducing(802) the(803) same(804) absolute(805) rule(806) into(807) these(808) colonies(809) for(810) taking(811) away(812) our(813) charters(814) abolishing(815) our(816) most(817) valuable(818) laws(819) and(820) altering(821) fundamentally(822) the(823) forms(824) of(825) our(826) governments(827) for(828) suspending(829) our(830) own(831) legislature(832) and(833) declaring(834) themselves(835) invested(836) with(837) power(838) to(839) legislate(840) for(841) us(842) in(843) all(844) cases(845) whatsoever(846) he(847) has(848) abdicated(849) government(850) here(851) by(852) declaring(853) us(854) out(855) of(856) his(857) protection(858) and(859) waging(860) war(861) against(862) us(863) he(864) has(865) plundered(866) our(867) seas(868) ravaged(869) our(870) coasts(871) burnt(872) our(873) towns(874) and(875) destroyed(876) the(877) lives(878) of(879) our(880) people(881) he(882) is(883) at(884) this(885) time(886) transporting(887) large(888) armies(889) of(890) foreign(891) mercenaries(892) to(893) complete(894) the(895) works(896) of(897) death(898) desolation(899) and(900) tyranny(901) already(902) begun(903) with(904) circumstances(905) of(906) cruelty(907) and(&)(908) perfidy(909) scarcely(910) paralleled(911) in(912) the(913) most(914) barbarous(915) ages(916) and(917) totally(918) unworthy(919) the(920) head(921) of(922) a(923) civilized(924) nation(925) he(926) has(927) constrained(928) our(929) fellow(930) citizens(931) taken(932) captive(933) on(934) the(935) high(936) seas(937) to(938) bear(939) arms(940) against(941) their(942) country(943) to(944) become(945) the(946) executioners(947) of(948) their(949) friends(950) and(951) brethren(952) or(953) to(954) fall(955) themselves(956) by(957) their(958) hands(959) he(960) has(961) excited(962) domestic(963) insurrections(964) amongst(965) us(966) and(967) has(968) endeavored(969) to(970) bring(971) on(972) the(973) inhabitants(974) of(975) our(976) frontiers(977) the(978) merciless(979) Indian(980) savages(981) whose(982) known(983) rule(984) of(985) warfare(986) is(987) an(988) undistinguished(989) destruction(990) of(991) all(992) ages(993) sexes(994) and(995) conditions(996) in(997) every(998) stage(999) of(1000) these(1001) oppressions(1002) we(1003) have(1004) petitioned(1005) for(1006) redress(1007) in(1008) the(1009) most(1010) humble(1011) terms(1012) our(1013) repeated(1014) petitions(1015) have(1016) been(1017) answered(1018) only(1019) by(1020) repeated(1021) injury(1022) a(1023) prince(1024) whole(1025) character(1026) is(1027) thus(1028) marked(1029) by(1030) every(1031) act(1032) which(1033) may(1034) define(1035) a(1036) tyrant(1037) is(1038) unfit(1039) to(1040) be(1041) the(1042) ruler(1043) of(1044) a(1045) free(1046) people(1047) nor(1048) have(1049) we(1050) been(1051) wanting(1052) in(1053) attention(1054) to(1055) our(1056) British(1057) brethren(1058) we(1059) have(1060) warned(1061) them(1062) from(1063) time(1064) to(1065) time(1066) of(1067) attempts(1068) by(1069) their(1070) legislature(1071) to(1072) extend(1073) an(1074) unwarrantable(1075) jurisdiction(1076) over(1077) us(1078) we(1079) have(1080) reminded(1081) them(1082) of(1083) the(1084) circumstances(1085) of(1086) our(1087) emigration(1088) and(1089) settlement(1090) here(1091) we(1092) have(1093) appealed(1094) to(1095) their(1096) native(1097) justice(1098) and(1099) magnanimity(1100) and(1101) we(1102) have(1103) conjured(1104) them(1105) by(1106) the(1107) ties(1108) of(1109) our(1110) common(1111) kindred(1112) to(1113) disavow(1114) these(1115) usurpations(1116) which(1117) would(1118) inevitably(1119) interrupt(1120) our(1121) connections(1122) and(1123) correspondence(1124) they(1125) too(1126) have(1127) been(1128) deaf(1129) to(1130) the(1131) voice(1132) of(1133) justice(1134) and(1135) of(1136) consanguinity(1137) we(1138) must(1139) therefore(1140) acquiesce(1141) in(1142) the(1143) necessity(1144) which(1145) denounces(1146) our(1147) separation(1148) and(1149) hold(1150) them(1151) as(1152) we(1153) hold(1154) the(1155) rest(1156) of(1157) mankind(1158) enemies(1159) in(1160) war(1161) in(1162) peace(1163) friends(1164) we(1165) therefore(1166) the(1167) representatives(1168) of(1169) the(1170) united(1171) states(1172) of(1173) America(1174) in(1175) general(1176) congress(1177) assembled(1178) appealing(1179) to(1180) the(1181) supreme(1182) judge(1183) of(1184) the(1185) world(1186) for(1187) the(1188) rectitude(1189) of(1190) our(1191) intentions(1192) do(1193) in(1194) the(1195) name(1196) and(1197) by(1198) authority(1199) of(1200) the(1201) good(1202) people(1203) of(1204) these(1205) colonies(1206) solemnly(1207) publish(1208) and(1209) declare(1210) that(1211) these(1212) united(1213) colonies(1214) are(1215) and(1216) of(1217) right(1218) ought(1219) to(1220) be(1221) free(1222) and(1223) independent(1224) states(1225) that(1226) they(1227) are(1228) absolved(1229) from(1230) all(1231) allegiance(1232) to(1233) the(1234) British(1235) crown(1236) and(1237) that(1238) all(1239) political(1240) connection(1241) between(1242) them(1243) and(1244) the(1245) state(1246) of(1247) great(1248) Britain(1249) is(1250) and(1251) ought(1252) to(1253) be(1254) totally(1255) dissolved(1256) and(1257) that(1258) as(1259) free(1260) and(1261) independent(1262) states(1263) they(1264) have(1265) full(1266) power(1267) to(1268) levy(1269) war(1270) conclude(1271) peace(1272) contract(1273) alliances(1274) establish(1275) commerce(1276) and(1277) to(1278) do(1279) all(1280) other(1281) acts(1282) and(1283) things(1284) which(1285) independent(1286) states(1287) may(1288) of(1289) right(1290) do(1291) and(1292) for(1293) the(1294) support(1295) of(1296) this(1297) declaration(1298) with(1299) a(1300) firm(1301) reliance(1302) on(1303) the(1304) protection(1305) of(1306) divine(1307) providence(1308) we(1309) mutually(1310) pledge(1311) to(1312) each(1313) other(1314) our(1315) lives(1316) our(1317) fortunes(1318) and(1319) our(1320) sacred(1321) honor(1322) .

"I furnish herewith a translation of Paper No. 2, indicating of what the treasure consists, based upon the use of the Declaration of Independence as the Key:

I h a v e d e p o s i t e d
115 73 24 818 37 52 49 17 31 62 657 22 7 15

i n t h e c o u n t y o f
140 47 29 107 79 84 56 238 10 26 822 5 195

B e d f o r d, a b o u t f o u r
308 85 52 159 136 49 210 36 0 46 316 543 122 106 95 53

m i l e s f r o m B u f o r d' s,
58 2 42 7 35 122 53 31 82 77 250 195 56 96 118 71

i n a n e x c a v a t i o n
140 287 28 353 37 994 65 147 818 24 3 8 12 47

o r v a u l t, s i x f e e t
43 59 818 45 316 101 41 78 154 994 122 138 190 16

b e l o w t h e s u r f a c e
77 49 107 57 72 34 73 85 35 371 59 195 81 92 190

o f t h e g r o u n d, t h e
106 273 60 394 629 270 219 106 388 287 63 3 6 190

f o l l o w i n g a r t i c l e s,
122 43 233 400 106 290 314 47 48 81 96 26 115 92 157 190 110

B e l o n g i n g j o i n t l y
77 85 195 46 10 113 140 353 48 120 106 2 607 61 420 822

T o t h e p a r t i e s w h o s e
29 125 14 20 37 105 28 248 16 158 7 35 19 301 125 110 496

n a m e s a r e g i v e n
287 98 117 520 62 51 219 37 113 140 818 138 549

i n n u m b e r t h r e e
8 44 287 388 117 18 79 344 34 20 59 520 557

h e r e w i t h .
107 612 219 37 66 154 41 20

T h e f i r s t d e p o s i t
50 6 584 122 154 248 110 61 52 33 30 5 38 8 14

c o n s i s t e d o f t e n
84 57 549 216 115 71 29 85 63 43 131 29 138 47

h u n d r e d a n d f o u r t e e n
73 238 549 52 53 79 118 51 44 63 195 12 238 112 3 49 79 353

p o u n d s o f g o l d
105 56 371 565 210 515 125 360 133 143 101 15

a n d t h i r t y - e i g h t
284 549 252 14 204 140 344 26 822 138 115 48 73 34

h u n d r e d a n d t w e l v e
204 316 616 63 219 7 52 150 44 52 16 40 37 157 818 37

p o u n d s o f s i l v e r
121 12 95 10 15 35 12 131 62 115 102 818 49 53

d e p o s i t e d N o v
135 138 30 31 62 67 41 85 63 10 106 818

e i g h t e e n n i n e t e e n
138 8 113 20 32 33 37 353 287 140 47 85 50 37 49 47

T h e s e c o n d w a s
64 6 7 71 33 4 43 47 63 1 27 609

m a d e D e c e i g h t e e n
207 229 15 190 246 85 94 520 2 270 20 39 7 33 44

t w e n t y - o n e , a n d
22 40 7 10 3 822 106 44 496 229 353 210

c o n s i s t e d o f
199 31 10 38 140 297 61 612 320 302 676

n i n e t e e n h u n d r e d
287 2 44 33 32 520 557 10 6 250 556 245 53 37 52

a n d s e v e n p o u n d s
83 47 320 38 33 818 7 44 30 31 250 10 15 35

o f g o l d a n d t w e l v e
106 159 113 31 102 406 229 549 320 29 66 33 101 818 138

h u n d r e d a n d e I g h t y -
301 316 353 320 219 37 52 28 549 320 33 8 49 107 50 822

e i g h t o f s i l v e r
7 2 113 73 16 125 11 110 67 102 818 33 59

a l s o j e w e l s
81 157 38 43 590 138 19 85 400 38

o b t a i n e d i n S t
43 77 14 27 8 47 138 63 140 44 33 22

L o u i s i n e x c h a n g e
176 106 250 314 216 2 10 7 994 4 20 25 44 48 7

t o s a v e t r a n s -
26 46 110 229 818 190 34 112 147 44 110 -

p o r t a t i o n , a n d
121 125 96 41 51 50 140 56 47 152 549 63

v a l u e d a t t h i r t e e n
818 28 42 250 138 591 98 653 32 107 140 112 26 85 138 549

T h e a b o v e i s
14 20 7 24 18 13 818 37 67 110

s e c u r e l y p a c k e d
62 33 21 95 219 520 102 822 30 83 84 305 620 15

i n i r o n p o t s
2 10 8 219 106 353 105 106 60 242

w i t h i r o n c o v e r s .
72 9 50 204 184 112 125 549 65 105 818 190 95 110

T h e v a u l t i s
16 73 53 818 150 409 400 50 154 285

r o u g h l y l i n e d
96 106 316 270 204 101 822 400 8 44 37 52

w i t h s t o n e a n d
40 240 34 204 38 16 46 47 85 24 44 15

t h e v e s s e l s r e s t
64 73 138 818 85 78 410 33 420 515 53 37 38 22

o n s o l i d s t o n e
31 10 110 106 101 140 15 38 3 5 44 7

a n d a r e c o v e r e d
98 287 135 150 96 33 84 125 818 190 96 520 118

w i t h o t h e r s.
459 370 653 466 106 41 107 612 219 275

P a p e r n u m b (e r) o n e
30 150 105 49 53 287 250 207 134 753 12 47 85
d e s c r i b e s t h e
63 138 110 21 112 140 495 496 515 12 47 85

e x a c t l o c a l i t y o f
584 994 150 199 16 42 5 4 25 42 8 16 822 125 159

t h e v a u l t s o t h a t
32 204 612 818 81 95 405 41 609 136 14 20 28 26

n o d i f f i c u l t y
353 302 246 8 131 159 140 84 440 42 16 822

w i l l b e h a d I n
40 67 101 102 193 138 204 51 63 240 549

f i n d i n g i t.
122 8 10 63 140 47 48 140 288

In preparing cipher No.2 Beale used the initial letter of each numbered word referred to, except,-

Word 822, fundamentally, he used the final letter, y.
Word 994, sexes, he used the medial letter, x.
Word 95, inalienable is spelled by Thomas Jefferson with a "u", so that Beale properly found a word in the Declaration of Independence beginning with "u".

"In conclusion it may not be inappropriate to say a few words regarding myself: In consequence of the time lost in the above investigation, I have been reduced from comparative affluence to absolute penury, entailing suffering upon those it was my duty to protect, and this, too, in spite of their remonstrances. My eyes were at last opened to their condition, and I resolved to sever at once, and forever, all connection with the affair, and retrieve, if possible, my errors. To do this, as the best means of placing temptation beyond my reach, I determined to make public the whole matter, and shift from my shoulders my responsibility to Mr. Morriss.

"I anticipate for these papers a large circulation, and, to avoid the multitude of letters with which I should be assailed from all sections of the Union, propounding all sorts of questions, and requiring answers which, if attended to, would absorb my entire time, and only change the character of my work, I have decided upon withdrawing my name from the publication, after assuring all interested that I have given all that I know of the matter, and that I cannot add one word to the statements herein contained.

"The gentleman whom I have selected as my agent, to publish and circulate these papers, was well-known to Mr. Morriss; it was at his house that Mrs. Morriss died, and he would have been one of the beneficiaries in the event of my success. Like every one else, he was ignorant of this episode in Mr. Morriss' career, until the manuscript was placed in his hands. Trusting that he will be benefited by the arrangement, which, I know, would have met the approval of Mr. Morriss, I have left the whole subject to his sole management and charge. It is needless to say that I shall await with much anxiety the development of the mystery."

(*And thus endeth what was contained in the printed pamphlet prepared by James B. Ward, of Campbell County, Virginia, practically all copies of which pamphlet were destroyed by fire which broke out in the plant of the Virginian Job Print, Lynchburg, Va., before a plan of sale had been carried out.*)

Now Geo. I. Hart resumes where he left off in his forward to this typewritten account of the Beale Papers:

When my brother Clayton secured a copy of the printed pamphlet containing Ward's story about the Beale papers, I think in the summer of 1898, he asked me to read same two or three times and then sit down and discuss the subject with him. This I did. We were at a loss to know how to begin any new or untried effort to unravel the mystery.

That Ward, by accident as he suggests, succeeded in finding a key to cipher No. 2, outlining the number of pounds of gold and silver, along with jewels of a value of $13,000, claimed to have been buried, created a suspicion that the story might have been made up instead of founded on fact, with the idea of finding a more ready sale of the pamphlet. Beale's letter to Mr. Moriss, accompanying the ciphers, did not state which of the three ciphers described the place of concealment, but one would think that cipher No.1 would be the starting point and have the most attention.

And why would Beale go to the trouble to prepare three ciphers, each based upon a different document?

If the story was not based upon fact but something prepared with the idea of making money from the sale of it, why was it allowed to remain in the printing plant until an accidental fire consumed practically all copies of it?

I suggested that my brother Clayton make a trip to Lynchburg and secure any information within reach, visiting Ward if he could locate him. He made several trips, and inquired all around the town, becoming convinced that it was more than probably the story was founded upon fact.

Thereupon Clayton redoubled his efforts to find a key, or keys, to ciphers No.1 and No.3. He worked every night for upwards of two years without making any headway, but, like Ward, was unwilling to lay the subject aside.

Having studied hypnotism and mesmerism, which had become somewhat of a fad in Roanoke about that time, as a result of several demonstrations on the stage of the Academy of Music, Clayton began to try out his powers on numerous promising subjects. Finding one exceptionally good subject, in the person of an eighteen-year-old lad in the neighborhood of our old home, Hagnolia, on the extreme northern line of the City of Roanoke, Va., he, after a time, tried out as a crystal reader or clairvoyant.

To Clayton's astonishment the boy, while in a state of trance, related a wonderful story, one which fitted in so well with what he had learned about the treasure that he determined to unravel the mystery, if possible, through that means. So he invited me to witness a séance and tell him what I thought of what I would see and hear.

The subject was a quiet, unassuming, different boy. In his normal state he seemed quite effeminate, and never indulged in the use of profane language. Under the spell, however, he seemed transformed into a vigorous, determined man of the world, confident of himself, swearing blandly, and ready to meet all comers. The following is an account of that incident, written by me some ten years thereafter at the request of my brother Clayton. I had no note matthete, so the account came purely from memory—and may be more or less inaccurate. However, the following depicts the occurrence as I remembered it, with Clayton acting as interrogator, I being merely a quiet listener and observer.

A CRYSTAL READING.

"Jewels, By Gosh! Diamonds! Rubies! Pearls! Emeralds! Whew! Ain't the old man rich?"

These and other similar exclamations came from the lips of medium as he gazed into the crystal ball. Oblivious of his surroundings, apparently in a trance, eyes bulging, features tense, a death-like grip on what was opaque to the bystanders, but which, when revolved in the hands of the medium, like the earth on its axis, seemed an inspiration, the clairvoyant quickly turned back the pages of time to a century before, and claimed to read events then taking place. I stepped into the dimly lighted room, on the second floor of our old home, Magnolia, Just after the medium had entered the state of trance, and while my brother, Clayton, was commanding:

"Time is moving backward quite fast, and will continue so moving until you reach November 1819. Go to Buford's Tavern, in a village of that name just to the east of the Blue Ridge Mountains, and watch for the coming of several prairie schooners. Tell me as soon as the come in sight, and relate everything that those in charge do. Now, tell me everything they have with them, and don't let them get out of your sight!"

Within about thirty seconds the medium straightened up, and, trembling as if from the excitement, began to talk:

"Here they come! They're just passing through the gap in the mountain."

"Watch them carefully! Don't let them get out of your sight! How many wagons or prairie schooners do you see?"

"I see five covered wagons."

"Are there any men riding horses, or mules, accompanying the wagons?"

"Yes; five men on hourses."

"How many men are there altogether?"

"Let me see? (As if counting on his fingers) There's ten; five men driving the wagons and five men on horseback."

"Where are they riding in reference to the wagons, by the side of the wagons, or in the rear of the wagons?"

"A big, fine looking fellow is riding alone in front, two men are riding abreast just in his rear, followed by the five men driving the wagons, and two men are riding abreast at the rear of the wagons."

"Have the men any guns or pistols?"

"Sure! Each man riding horseback has a rifle slung across the front of his saddle, with two pistols in leather containers slung from his belt, one to his right hand, the other to his left hand."

"Each driver has a rifle and a couple of pistols on the seat beside him. Oh! They're fixed for game, and I reckon, for Indians, Too!"

"Watch them carefully and tell me if they stop anywhere?"

There was silence for a minute or two, when Clayton stepped up the time with a command.

"They've stopped."

"Where?"

"At a place that has a board up over the door and on it marked "Tavern". And, on a little building right by the side of it, I see another board which says "Bufford Post Office". And I see a few other houses scattered about."

"Watch them carefully, now, and tell me everything they do."

"The big fellow, the one who was riding in front, and I guess he is the boss of the outfit, has done got off his horse and handed the reins to another fellow, and gone into the tavern."

"Watch them closely and tell me all that is done."

"The boss is talking to same man inside the tavern. I guess he's asking can he take care of his men and horses. Anyhow the tavern-keeper smiles and bows his head, pushing forward a much-worn book, The boss man is writing in it."

"What are they doing now?"

"They are driving around to the stable. The boss man has taken his saddlebags off his horse, turned the birdle reins over to an old gray-haired negro, and has done gone into the tavern."

"Don't let him get out of your sight! Watch him closely, and tell me all that he does!"

"The boss man is done gone upstairs. It's nearly dark. A negro slave is showing him to a room. But the big fellow wouldn't as if he thinks it's mighty unusual for a gentleman. I guess in those days negro slaves were expected to do everything for the guest except spit."

"Well, never mind about your wise cracks. Keep a close watch on the big fellow! Don't let him out of your sight! What is he doing?"

"He's done raised the window and is motioning to one of his pals, who is out in the yard, to come up to his room. That fellow is now going up the steps, and is entering the room. The boss man is talking, motioning to his saddle bags, and is now going back down the steps, while the other man stays in the room. He's done gone in and sat down at the supper table."

"Time is passing a little faster now. Tell me what the boss man, as you term him, is doing."

"He's done gone back upstairs to his room. He's motioning the other fellow to go to the room; I guess he's telling him to go downstairs and get his grub."

"Watch the boss man carefully, now, and tell me everything he does. Time is passing more slowly, remember!"

"The boss man is pulling down the shades. My! Those shades are on strings; the don't roll down like shades do nowadays, on springs. He's stuffing some paper into the keyhole. No wonder, for the keyhole is almost as big as three fingers of a man's hand. The key must be mighty big. Yes, it is, for I see it there on the table."

"Well go along and tell me what the man is doing."

"Now he's putting his old big pistol on the table, right by the side of the candle. He's laying his saddlebags across the bed, and is __ both sides. I wonder if he is hunting for a bottle of rum?"

"Never mind about any bottle. Watch that man closely, and tell me everything he does?"

"My God! The old man is opening up a regular diamond mine! They glitter so they hurt my eyes. I didn't know there was so many fine jewels in all the world. It beats any jeweler's show case I ever saw."

"Tell me about what he has. What do you see?"

"Jewels, By Gosh! Diamonds! Rubies! Pearls! Emeralds! Whew! Ain't that beg fellow some pumpkins?"

And the subject shaded his eyes with his hands, as though the brilliance of the precious stones was dazzling him; and, all the while he was turning his head to right and to left, as if either to see more or to shake away the sight he was beholding.

"Keep close watch on the big fellow and tell me everything he does", Clayton amonished."

"Now, he's wrapping up the jewels in something that looks like fine skins, and putting them back into his saddlebags. He's putting the saddlebags under the pillow, between featherbed and pillows, and has thrown the bolster off onto a chair. He's reading the bible, which was lying on the table."

"Time is passing more quickly now. Tell me what the boss man, as you call him, does before he snuffs out the candle?"

"He's done replaced the bible on the table. He's snuffing out the candle. The room is now dark."

"Go out to the stable and tell me what is being done by his companions out there?" Clayton suggested.

"The horses are in stalls, munching hay. The five prairie cow stable. There's a man sitting in each wagon, the men being, in each case, in front of one wagon and in the rear of the adjoining wagon. Each man has two pistols in his belt, with a rifle at his side. Now, that's darn funny; why don't they go in the tavern and go to bed?"

"If you'll keep your shirt on maybe we will find out. Where are the other four men?"

"Oh! They've done gone to bed in the tavern."

"Look through the prairie schooners carefully and tell me what you find?"

"What do you expect me to find? You ain't got nothing to do with them damned, all-fired wagons!"

"Never mind about that. You don't have to look after the welfare of those men; they're well able to protect themselves.

You just go ahead and look in each wagon, one after the other, and tell me what you find."

"In the first one there is some hay, corn and straw, and--"

Thereupon the medium slowed down, and, with mouth open wide but tongue stilled, turned his head one way and then another, while his eyes, opened wider than usual, were glued to the crystal.

"Tell me what you see?" commanded Clayton."

"Two iron pots! They are covered with a blanket, and are buried under straw."

"What do you see in the pots?"

"Great God! Just look at the gold! And silver, too! Geeminy cracked corn, I don't wonder they have so many shooting irons ready for instant use."

"Look in the next wagon and tell me what you see there."

"Oh! There's just some skins of wild animals, some jerked meat, a blanket or two, and some hay and straw."

"Look more carefully. Are you sure there is nothing else in that wagon?"

"Well, I should s-a-y not! There's two more pots in that gol-darned wagon."

"Tell me what is in them."

"Silver! Good Lord, I didn't know there was so much silver in one place anywhere in the world. They are filled with silver. And the fellow watching that prairie schooner has just kicked them, I guess to make sure they're still there."

"Isn't there any gold in either of those pots?"

"No. God damn it to hell, do you think they'd mix gold and silver. And I just want to warn you, that boss man ain't going to let anybody come near. So you keep away."

"Never mind about that. I just want you to tell me everything you find in those wagons. Now, go on to the third prairie schooner and look that over carefully."

"Well, I see some more corn and hay—and, I believe, there are some oats. Yes, that's right. And there are some animal skins. I guess that fellow hasn't got a blanket. And he was nodding, too, and his pal in the next wagon told him to wake up and keep his eyes open."

"Isn't there anything else in that wagon?"

"I don't see anything else."

"Look more carefully, from one end of the wagon to the other."

"Well! Well! If I don't beat the old scratch! Sure! There's another old iron pot in that wagon, but it was so well covered up that I thought there was just coon skin coats."

"what is in the pot?"

"My goodness alive! Ain't there no end to this thing? Why it contains silver, nothing but silver. I wonder what they're going to do with all this gold and silver?"

"Go on to the fourth prairie-schooner and tell me what you find in it?"

"That old fellow is fast asleep, leaning against the top. He better wake up before the boss man in the tavern catches up with him, for I'll be he'd skin him alive."

"Never mind, for the moment, the boss man in the tavern. Do you find anything unusual in that wagon?"

"No. Just some hey, and corn, and straws, and skins. Also some camping utensils. And I believe, there's a tent or two in there."

"All right. Now go on to the last wagon. What, if anything of interest, do you find there?"

"Just the same kinds of things. More corn and hay and oats. And I see some Indian trinkets, some Indian bows and arrows. That's all. "All right. Let everything be natural with you for a time. You are at ease. I think you need a rest. We will have some eats before we resume out travel along the old trail."

Thereupon, Clayton and I, and the subject, repaired to the other end of the room, and ate what Clayton had prepared for our use before beginning the séance. The boy being at ease, resumed his usual demeanor, rather different and retiring, with little to say even when asked a question. When interrogated about what had transpired during the séance, he seemed to recall nothing.

The repast being disposed of, Clayton again hypnotized the subject, handed to him the crystal ball, and the séance was resumed.

"Now, time is passing very fast until you get back to November 1819, and reach Buford's Tavern, fourteen miles east of here, to the east of the Blue Ridge Mountains. Tell me what you find being done about Buford's Tavern?"

After a few moments hesitation, the subject said:

"Why, there is the boss man, out there on a horse. And, you bet, he has them saddlebags strapped securely onto the rear of his saddle. One of his pals is leaving the first wagon and coming up to him. He's getting on a horse, too."

"Well, watch them carefully and tell me where they go and what they do."

"There they go, out to the right, over towards the mountain, but to the south."

"How many men are in this party?"

"Only two; the Boss man, as he seems to be, and one of his pals."

Well, watch them carefully, now, and tell me where they go and what they do?"

"They're riding along an old rutty road, more like a trail than a real road. Now they're leaving the road and following a path up into the edge of the mountain."

"Watch them, and tell me everything they do."

"Well ain't I doing it? They've gotten off their horses. They're going into a cave. They've candles with them. They've lighted their candles and are examining the cave. They've found some potatoes and other vegetables, and the men shake their heads, as if surprised and disappointed. They're snuffing their candles at the edge of the cave. They're getting on their horses again and are starting back toward the tavern."

"Looks like midday. The sun is right overhead. The boss man is looking up at it."

"Well, tell me what they do next, especially when they get back to the tavern. Time is hurrying along."

"They're back at the tavern. The negro slave has taken the boss man's horse, also the other man's horse. The boss man and his pal have gone into the tavern, and up to the boss man's room. The boss man is shaking his head."

"Very well, time is fast passing along. Tell me when their next move is made."

"Roosters are crowing. I see the first streaks of dawn resting on the Peaks of Otter. The boss man is lighting his candle. He's now slipping on his trousers, and putting on his boots. He's putting his belt around his waist, and adjusting his pistols. Now he's grabbing up his saddlebags, and is going down the steps of the tavern."

"Watch carefully. Tell me all he does."

"Bless my soul, do you know, what that negro slave was out currying and saddling and bridling the boss man's horse. There he is, leading the horse around to the front of the tavern. The boss man is adjusting his saddlebags, and the negro slave is having trouble to hold the horse, who seems to be prancing to be off. Now the boss man is aside his horse, and is starting off north, to the left of the Peaks of Otter."

"Watch him carefully, and tell me all that he does."

"There he goes, the horse in a fox trot, along the trail which borders Goose Creek and landing to a gap in the Blue Ridge not far from the Twin Peaks. It is on the trail which runs from Bedford County across the mountain to Botetourt County. There's occasionally a house, with a little cleared land around it, but for the most part the hills are covered with forest trees. How the boss man is leaving the trail, is riding off into the woods, but is shaking his head, as if he doesn't like what he sees; and goes back to the trail again."

"Keep close watch on the boss man, as you term him. Tell me all that he does."

"He's again leaving the trail, crossing a little branch, and going through the woods, up a little hill. Well, isn't that a strange place—a small hill, with a cup-like formation or indentation in it, all covered with giant trees. The boss man is looking around carefully. He's hitched his horse to the limb of a tree, and now is examining the place, as if he's hunting for something. He must like what he has found, for he is smiling. He's knocking the bark off a spot on a big oak tree with the butt of one of his pistols, and now he's cutting the spot more deeply with his hunting knife. He's on his horse again, and is returning to the tavern."

"Watch him carefully, and tell me anything unusual that he may do. Time is passing faster, and tell me when the boss man reaches the tavern."

"He's done got back to the tavern. The negro slave's out ready to serve the boss man. The boss man throws him the bridle rein, grabs his saddlebags, and walks into the dining room. Yes, and he's laid his saddlebags carefully under the chair and set his foot on the leather connecting the two bags. He ain't taking no chances with losing them jewels, and I don't blame him."

"Well time is passing a little faster. Skip over the more unimportant details, and tell me what is done by the boss man and his associates."

"It's the next morning. The wagon train is starting off just like it arrived at the tavern, except that the rifles are in the wagons and the horsemen only have their pistols in their belts. They're waving, apparently a good bye, to the tavern keeper."

"Which way are they going?"

"The same way the boss man went on his trip horseback the morning before. He's talking to the two men in front, and pointing to the Peaks of Otter."

"Time is speeding along. Tell me where they go."

"They are following the same route the boss man went yesterday morning. There, they're having a little trouble fording the branch. Now they're going along the creek, and have stopped where the boss man went up the hill. I don't believe the teams can get up the hill. Ho, they can't. The boss man's pointing and talking. They're carrying the pots up the hill. My! Those pots must be heavy. Now they're carrying picks and shovels up the hill."

"Where are they placing the pots?"

"Close by the foot of the giant oak that the boss man chipped bark off of when he was there before. Now they're digging, taking turns at the job."

"Time is passing faster. Tell me what is finally done with the pots."

"You're mighty impatient! Why don't you let me take my time to see and tell you about the whole job?"

"We don't care about all the details. We just want to know what was finally done with the pots."

"Well, they've dug a hole about as deep as a man is tall. It's about the size of a grave, except it's wider and rounder. They've hunted up a lot of flat stones and paved the bottom of the hole, and set the pots on the stones, and then covered the pots with more stones. They're filling the hole with the earth taken from it, carefully soothing over the top, and spreading leaves over the fresh earth."

"Tell me everything they do."

"All the men have gone back to the wagons, except the boss man. He's cutting a larger place in the tree, a marker I reckon. Well, what a fool! The boss man pulled something like flour out of his pocket and threw it on the freshly cut place. Now the boss man is making some marks on a paper, looks like a sort of diagram. He's done and is joining the other fellows, who had moved down the trail. Now they're on their way back down the creek, the way they came."

"Time is passing faster. Tell me when they stop anywhere."

"They've reached the tavern, and the boss man is talking to the tavern keeper. He seems to be welcomed. The horses are being unhitched."

"Time is passing faster now. Tell me what they do when they make their next move."

"Well, it is next morning, after breakfast. Seven of the men, with the five wagons and two saddle horses, are starting off east, along the well-traveled road. The boss man and two of his pals, are remaining."

"Time is passing faster now. Watch the three men and tell me if they go anywhere near the buried treasure, or when they take their departure in any direction."

"The boss man and his two pals seem to be sticking around the neighborhood, riding around during the day, and occasionally entering into conversation with the villagers after supper."

"Time is hurrying along. Jump over everything until the boss man, as you term him, or one of his associates, makes a move to leave the tavern."

"It's now the end of about three weeks. The boss man is biding the tavern keeper good bye. They are on their horses and are heading east."

"Well, that is enough for the present. You may be at rest. We may resume our travels some time later."

Thereupon the subject seemed let down. He resumed his former demeanor, different and uninterested in anything about him. He was thanked for his visit, and left Magnolia, going in the direction of his home.

My brother, Clayton, and I discussed the séance, not believing anything that had transpired, and, still, wondering if there could be the possibility of some truth in what the subject had blurted forth.

Now, in conclusion:

Not being present at a later séance, when Clayton attempted to get from the subject what had happened to Beale and his 29 associates, I can only state, in a few words, what Clayton told me about it: That, when gazing into the crystal ball, he asked the subject to follow the party of 10 west, after their second trip to the States, and have them join the 20 left behind to continue searching for gold and silver, and keep with the entire party until, either they returned to their homes, or were no more, the subject, in a most realistic but shocked manner, detailed their being set upon Indians, as they were preparing to leave their operations, when all were killed and scalped.

And this endeth a weird and almost unbelievable story.

Notes

Notes

www.ingramcontent.com/pod-product-compliance
Lightning Source LLC
Chambersburg PA
CBHW071315060426
42444CB00036B/3045
9781952658013